IMPOSSIBLE ESCAPE

A TRUE STORY OF SURVIVAL AND HEROISM IN NAZI GERMANY

STEVE SHEINKIN

ROARING BROOK PRESS

New York

Published by Roaring Brook Press

Roaring Brook Press is a division of

Holtzbrinck Publishing Holdings Limited Partnership

120 Broadway, New York, NY 10271 • fiercereads.com

Maps on pp. 2–3, 64, and 188 by Anna Frohmann

Maps on pp. 52 and 121 courtesy of the United States Holocaust Memorial
Museum Photo Archives; copyright of United States Holocaust Memorial Museum

Our books may be purchased in bulk for promotional, educational, or business
use. Please contact your local bookseller or the Macmillan Corporate and
Premium Sales Department at (800) 221-7945 ext. 5442 or by email at
MacmillanSpecialMarkets@macmillan.com.

Library of Congress Cataloging-in-Publication Data

Names: Sheinkin, Steve, author.

Title: Impossible escape : a true story of survival and heroism in Nazi Europe /
Steve Sheinkin.

Description: First. | New York, NY : Roaring Brook Press, [2023] | Includes index.
Audience: Ages 12–18 | Audience: Grades 10–12

Summary: "From award-winning author Steve Sheinkin, a true story of two
Jewish teenagers racing against time during the Holocaust—one in hiding in
Hungary, and the other in Auschwitz, plotting escape"—Provided by publisher.

Identifiers: LCCN 2023018607 | ISBN 9781250265722 (hardcover)

Subjects: LCSH: Holocaust, Jewish (1939–1945)—Europe—Juvenile literature.
Jews—Persecutions—Europe—Juvenile literature.

Classification: LCC D804.34 .S537 2023 | DDC 940.53/18—dc23/eng/20230426

LC record available at https://lccn.loc.gov/2023018607

First edition, 2023

Book design by Aurora Parlagreco

Printed in the United States of America

ISBN 978-1-250-26572-2

3   5   7   9   10   8   6   4   2

In memory of my bubbe,
Anna Novis Sheinkin

CONTENTS

PROLOGUE
LEAVING HOME

"TAKE CARE OF YOURSELF," HIS mother said as he got into the taxi. "And don't forget to change your socks."

The car pulled from the curb. In the back seat, Rudi tore the yellow Star of David from the sleeve of his jacket. Jewish citizens of Slovakia were required to wear the star in public.

This was the first law he would break that night.

He ducked below the window, his heart pounding into his ribs, as the driver sped out of town and across the flat farmland to the south. Rudi had a little cash in his pocket. He had a box of matches, a compass, and some clothes in a small travel bag. Not much for the epic trek he planned.

But he was seventeen. He felt invincible.

After thirty minutes on dark roads, Rudi saw the glow of street-lights up ahead, and snow falling through the light. He sat up, grabbing his bag, as the car stopped in the small city of Sered.

The fare, said the driver, was 400 crowns.

Rudi had 200 crowns, total. And that was supposed to last him all the way to Great Britain.

He held out his cash, all of it.

The driver studied the money, pulling at the tip of his mustache.

"You'd better keep half," the man said, looking at his young passenger. "You're going to need it."

Rudi pocketed the money. As the taxi drove away, he stood in the falling snow, looking around.

Warm lights in café windows.

Groups of people at tables. Drinking, talking, laughing.

A policeman on patrol, coming his way.

Rudi turned and strode to the edge of town, toward the fields and woods along the border of Hungary. That was step one: slip across the border to Hungary. From there, his plan was to continue south, cross into German-occupied Yugoslavia, make his way down to the sea, find some way to board a boat to Britain, and join up to fight against Adolf Hitler.

Rudi's mother had tried to talk sense to him. This was March 1942, two and a half years into World War II. Germany had conquered most of Europe. Hitler's forces were rounding up young Jewish men, shipping them to unknown destinations. How could Rudi hope to stay hidden? How could he cross all those borders?

But Rudi was seventeen. Invincible.

His mother had stopped arguing. She'd gathered every cent she could spare from her dressmaking business and handed it all to her son. She'd even suggested the taxi. It was the quickest way to get near the border, and probably safe, if the driver kept his mouth shut.

Well, so far so good. Rudi made it out of town. When he was sure he was alone, he stopped and struck a match and held the flame to the face of his compass. He was headed in the right direction.

It was a smooth start to what would prove to be a journey into hell.

PART I
CAPTURE

FINLAND

Ielsinki

Tallinn

ESTONIA

Riga

LATVIA

UANIA

ovno

Minsk

BELARUS
(USSR)

Kiev

UKRAINE
(USSR)

ND

ROMANIA

Bucharest

BULGARIA

Sofia

RUSSIA
(USSR)

Moscow

Black Sea

Caspian Sea

Ankara

TURKEY

PERSIA

CE

SYRIA

IRAQ

CYPRUS

Damascus

1

RUDI *WOULD* FIND A WAY to fight Adolf Hitler. It can be said, without risk of exaggeration, that he would go on to be—while still a teenager—one of the great heroes of the entire Second World War.

But not in a way he ever could have imagined.

Growing up in the Central European country of Czechoslovakia, Rudolf Vrba's life was pretty good. Pretty normal. He liked school, especially science. He and his friends—some Jewish, some Christian—went to movies and soccer matches.

Sure, Rudi was aware of Europe's long history of prejudice against Jews. He'd hear the occasional antisemitic joke in the market—someone would be bargaining with a merchant, and they'd say, "What are you? A Jew or a human?"

It was ignorant and cruel. But this too was normal. All part of life for a Jewish kid.

Rudi was aware of Adolf Hitler, of course. No one could avoid hearing about Hitler, the fascist leader in Germany with the little square mustache, ranting and raving about Jews, vowing to make

Germany a great power again, demanding territory from neighbors, constantly threatening war. But this seemed far off. It didn't directly impact Rudi's world.

Until suddenly it did.

Born in Austria in 1889, Adolf Hitler fought for Germany in the First World War before jumping into extreme right-wing politics in his early thirties. Hitler and his Nazi Party competed in German elections throughout the 1920s and into the early 1930s. Even with Nazi thugs stalking the streets, intimidating voters and journalists, beating up political rivals, Hitler never won a majority of the national vote. But in a country badly divided between rival parties, he had one of the largest blocs of voters. He became chancellor of Germany in 1933, and from there moved quickly to seize the powers of a dictator.

Hitler banned other political parties. He shut down opposition newspapers. Less than two months after taking power, the Nazis established their first concentration camp, Dachau, in an old factory outside of Munich. Other camps followed: Sachsenhausen, Buchenwald, and Ravensbrück, where women were imprisoned. The Nazis used these camps to terrorize anyone deemed an "enemy of the state," anyone who didn't fit Hitler's vision of German society—a long list that included union leaders, communists, gay men, and Jews.

The camp system was run by Hitler's Schutzstaffel, or "protection squad"—known as the SS. The SS began as Hitler's private guard and expanded to a 250,000-member armed force that obeyed no rule of law other than the orders of the German dictator.

All the while, Hitler hammered away at what he called the

"Jewish question" and the "Jewish problem." He relentlessly attacked Jews as "subhuman," comparing them to a contagious disease, labeling them an inferior race with no place in Germany's future. He blamed Jews for Germany's loss in the First World War, for its economic hardships, for everything.

This was plainly preposterous. Jewish Germans, who made up less than 1 percent of the country's population, had fought and died in World War I at the same rate as non-Jews. Jewish scientists, including Albert Einstein, had brought ten Nobel Prizes home to Germany in the quarter century before Hitler took power.

But Hitler's rants were never meant to be logical. The goal was to unite a large group of people by turning them against a smaller, more vulnerable group. A typical tactic of tyrants.

With absolute power in his hands, Hitler stripped German Jews of their citizenship and rights. Jewish professors were banned from teaching. German universities started teaching absurd "racial science," which conveniently concluded that Germans were a "master race" and destined to build an empire in Europe.

In the late 1930s, Adolf Hitler began following through on his vow to expand Germany's borders. Hitler annexed Austria in 1938, then demanded that a huge part of Czechoslovakia come under German rule. France and Great Britain had the military strength to stop Hitler. But this was just twenty years after the end of the First World War, which had devastated an entire generation of young men. Unwilling to face the horrors of another European war, French and British leaders caved in to Hitler's demands. In early 1939, Hitler seized the Czech side of what had been Czechoslovakia.

Rudi's home, Slovakia, became an independent state. In theory.

In reality, the small country was dominated by Germany and led by a pro-Hitler president, Jozef Tiso.

This is when Rudi and his Jewish friends knew their world had changed.

Rudi's friend Gerta Sidonová was twelve in the summer of 1939. Gerta—or Gerti to her friends, but never Gertrúda, which she hated—was a thin girl with wavy blond hair and blue eyes. She loved to write and perform plays with her friends and dreamed of becoming a filmmaker.

One warm morning that summer, Gerta and a non-Jewish friend named Marushka rode their bicycles out of Trnava and along dirt roads between fields of ripening corn. After about an hour, they stopped to sit in the shade. They were talking about fishing later, about catching some of the flies buzzing around them for bait, when Marushka blurted out: "My father said I shouldn't have come out with you today."

Gerta was stunned. Marushka's father worked in Gerta's family's butcher shop. He'd always seemed like a nice man.

"Why not?" she asked.

Her friend blushed before answering. "He said that because you are Jews, you will soon be taken away, and then he will be able to take over your father's shop and we will move into your house." Until all that happened, Marushka explained, her family had to be careful not to be seen mixing too much with Jewish people.

Gerta didn't know what to say. She'd never thought of friends in terms of their religion.

Finally she asked, "And what do you think about this?"

"I don't know," Marushka said, looking out at the fields, avoiding her friend's eyes. "I'm confused and will miss you, but if it's going to make it difficult for my family that I have a Jewish friend, I'll have to stop seeing you."

"That isn't really what I meant," Gerta said. She wanted to know what Marushka thought of the idea that Jewish families should be thrown out of their homes and sent away.

Marushka launched into a recital of tired old stereotypes about Jews being obsessed with money and needing to learn the value of hard work. Gerta had heard this garbage before but had no idea her friend believed it. Marushka knew Gerta's mother woke at 5:00 a.m. to work in the family shop before heading off to a second job. Their friend Rudi's mother was a seamstress who made dresses in her living room. How could anyone say they needed to "learn" hard work?

Was Marushka just repeating things she heard her father say?

Was she tempted by the opportunity to move into Gerta's house?

To Gerta, the strangest part of the whole conversation happened when she grabbed her bicycle and was about to ride off. Marushka called out, "But today we could have enjoyed ourselves."

Too furious to respond, Gerta got on her bike and pedaled toward home.

2

ON SEPTEMBER 1, 1939, HITLER launched an invasion of Poland, igniting World War II.

Britain and France were bound by treaty to fight alongside their Polish allies—but they were unprepared for a major war. Hitler's forces overran the Polish capital of Warsaw by the end of the month.

In Slovakia, following Hitler's lead, the government enacted a series of anti-Jewish laws. Signs warned Jews not to enter movie theaters or sports stadiums. Jewish citizens had to be off the streets by eight at night. Laws restricted where they could live, where they could work, how far they could travel without special permission. The government assigned non-Jewish "advisers" to work in—and prepare to take over—Jewish-owned shops. Another law required Jews to wear a yellow Star of David in public, six inches in diameter, sewn onto their clothes with a specific number of stiches.

When they showed up for the first day of school, Jewish students were not allowed inside.

Gerta walked up to her school building—and found the gate locked. She stood outside with a small group of Jewish students, wondering what to do. They'd been attending classes here for years. They knew all the teachers. But when they banged on the gate, the only response came from children shouting:

"Jews out!"

Gerta was shocked to hear this from students. Friends, or so she'd thought.

"As our anger mounted, we felt that we just couldn't leave without some action," Gerta later recalled. She went around to the back of the building, where students left their bicycles, and stuck sharp pebbles between the metal rims and rubber tires of the bike wheels.

This was not very satisfying, Gerta admitted.

"But it was something," she said. "It was a gesture to show that we would not accept without resistance what they did to us."

Jewish students were even ordered to turn in their school books. This was particularly painful for Rudi. He dropped off his textbooks and walked away, "glum and empty-handed," as he'd later say.

A friend of his, Erwin Eisler, came up beside him and whispered: "Don't worry. I've still got that chemistry book."

Rudi was impressed by this act of defiance. Grateful too; chemistry was his favorite subject. The two friends studied together when they could, sharing the forbidden text in the privacy of their homes.

Rudi turned fifteen that September. He kept himself busy by building a chemistry lab in a shed in his mother's garden. Gerta was among the friends who came over to visit Rudi's lab. He took contagious pleasure in explaining his experiments, describing why different substances changed color or texture when combined.

When he could find jobs, Rudi worked as a laborer. At night he studied at home, teaching himself Russian in the family living room. He had a knack for languages and a prodigious memory—he already spoke Slovak, Czech, Hungarian, and German. Rudi's mother teased him about his studies. What was a Jewish boy from Slovakia going to do with Russian?

She could never have guessed how it was going to help him.

On warm evenings, before curfew, Rudi, Gerta, and their friends met in a meadow outside of town. They'd sit together in the tall grass and talk about books and politics, about the terrifying state of the world and what they'd do if they were in charge.

Gerta found herself falling for Rudi. "He had a round, friendly face and a winning smile," she'd recall. Rudi was always happy to tutor Gerta in math and science, but he didn't seem to return the crush. She'd later find out that he was embarrassed by a hat she sometimes wore, which had a pom-pom and made her look, he thought, like a little kid.

"It is strange," she'd reflect. "Faced with all the really serious problems we had, we could nevertheless be affected by the same emotions as normal teenagers."

The teens' parents seemed to think Slovakia's surge of antisemitism would blow over. But to Rudi and Gerta's group of friends, this felt like more than a passing storm. Their Christian friends, kids they'd joked around with for years, wouldn't even look at them anymore. People threw bricks through their windows, scrawled "Jew" on the walls of their homes. Members of the Hlinka Guard—modeled on Hitler's dreaded SS—marched around in black uniforms and shiny boots, beating anyone they felt like beating.

Gerta told the group about the non-Jewish "adviser" assigned to her parents' butcher shop—Mr. Šimončič, the father of her former friend Marushka. The man openly robbed them. Far more chilling to Gerta was his utter lack of the slightest hint of shame.

As if all of this was perfectly normal.

"It will not be long now," he said to her, "and all of you will be gone."

Adolf Hitler's forces invaded western Europe in the spring of 1940, quickly overrunning Denmark, Norway, the Netherlands, Luxembourg, and France. Hitler turned east in June 1941, launching a massive attack on the Soviet Union. Millions of German troops drove deep into Soviet territory.

About 9.5 million Jewish people lived in Europe at this time— just under 2 percent of the continent's population. By the summer of 1941, nearly the entire Jewish population of Europe lived in territory under Hitler's control.

Throughout his years in power, Hitler had often declared his desire to expel Jews from Germany. Now he decided on a very different course of action.

Hitler issued his orders directly to Heinrich Himmler, head of the SS. A longtime member of Hitler's inner circle, Himmler was a rabid antisemite, with a square mustache like his idol's. "For him I could do anything," Himmler said of his boss. "Believe me, if Hitler were to say I should shoot my mother, I would do it and be proud of his confidence."

As German troops tore through Europe, Himmler's SS established new concentration camps in occupied territory. One of the largest was Auschwitz, built on the grounds of a former army base in southern Poland. The first prisoners at Auschwitz were Polish political opponents of Hitler.

That would change as the war continued to expand.

3

IN MID-1941, HEINRICH HIMMLER CALLED the kommandant of Auschwitz to Berlin for a meeting.

Himmler got right to business. "The Führer has given orders for the Final Solution of the Jewish question to be implemented," he told Kommandant Rudolf Höss, "and we—the SS—are to put those orders into practice."

Rudolf Höss, a forty-year-old SS officer, was not a particularly high-ranking Nazi. He did not understand why he was suddenly privy to Hitler's personal orders, or what was meant by "Final Solution."

Himmler made it perfectly clear. "The Jews are the eternal enemies of the German people," he said, "and must be wiped off the face of the earth. Now, during this war, all the Jews we can lay hands on are to be exterminated, without exception."

The Auschwitz concentration camp, Himmler explained, had a convenient combination of railroad access and isolation. Isolation was vital, as this "work" was to be done in absolute secret.

"It is to remain between the two of us," Himmler cautioned. "It is a hard and difficult job which requires your complete commitment, regardless of the difficulties which may arise."

World War II expanded again on December 7, 1941. Japan, which sided with Germany in the war, attacked the U.S. naval base at Pearl Harbor, Hawaii. This brought the United States into the conflict on the side of Great Britain, China, and the Soviet Union—the Allies.

But America was nowhere near ready for a global war. By the spring of 1942, U.S. forces were still mobilizing, and far from strong enough to challenge Hitler in Europe. The Soviets were fighting for their lives, backed to the outskirts of Moscow and other major Russian cities.

Germany was winning the war—and moving ahead with Hitler's "Final Solution."

The leaders of Slovakia agreed to help deport Slovak Jews. They even agreed to *pay* Germany for every Jew the Nazis took away. In return, Jozef Tiso's government insisted that the Jews must never return and that their homes and belongings would become the property of the state.

In early 1942, the Slovak government announced that Jewish citizens were going to be "resettled" in German-occupied Poland. Young Jewish men, ages sixteen to thirty, would go first. They were told they'd be put to work according to their skills, and their families would soon follow.

"Where do you think we will be sent?"

For Rudi and his friends, that was the main topic of conversation in the meadow.

"Into work camps," one of the teens guessed. "We will probably have to work very hard."

The friends had no way of knowing what "resettlement" really meant.

Still, Rudi had no intention of being plunked down in some labor camp and bossed around by a bunch of Nazis in shiny boots. This is when he decided to trek to Britain and join the fight against Hitler. This is when he left home in a taxi, hurried out of the city of Sered in the falling snow, and lit a match to check his compass.

He continued south toward the border, crossing into Hungary sometime after midnight.

Around five in the morning, caked with mud and eyes red with exhaustion, Rudi stood outside a large house in the town of Galanta, Hungary. It was far too early to knock on this family's front door.

But what choice did he have? He had to get off the street.

He knocked. No response.

He tried again, a little louder. Another wait.

Finally, footsteps. The door opened just a bit. A young woman peeked out. A maid? He saw fear in her eyes in the split second before she slammed the door.

Rudi looked over his shoulder, checking for passing police. He really had to get off the street. He held down the doorbell, making a long, obnoxious buzz.

The door opened. A woman in an elegant dressing gown glared at him, awaiting an explanation.

"I'm Rudi Vrba," he said. "A friend of Stefan's."

Stefan was a friend from school. He'd told Rudi about these relatives in Hungary, nice people who might help him.

"You'd better come in," the woman said.

Rudi stepped inside. He saw his reflection in a mirror on the wall.

"I'm sorry," he said. "I walked from Sered. I had to go through the fields."

"You mean . . ." The woman lowered her voice. "You came here illegally?"

He nodded.

She shook her head. He could see that she was considering options.

Finally she said, "You'd better have a bath."

The maid showed Rudi to a bathroom, even ran the water for him. He soaked in the hot soapy tub, feeling his body begin to relax. The first step of his quest was safely behind him.

4

AFTER HIS BATH, RUDI SAT down to breakfast with Stefan's relatives: the woman who'd let him in and her husband. They made pleasant small talk until Rudi was finished eating.

Then the man turned serious. "I suppose you know what conditions are like in Hungary?"

Rudi didn't, beyond the basics. He knew Hungary's authoritarian government had taken Hitler's side in the war, joining the Axis alliance, Germany's wartime pact with Italy and Japan. He knew Hungary had the same sorts of anti-Jewish laws as Slovakia—though, so far, they'd not been strictly enforced.

Yes, and there were other perils, the husband explained. Tensions between Hungary and Slovakia, long-standing disputes over territory, were running high. As far as Hungarian police were concerned, anyone illegally crossing the border was an enemy spy. Anyone helping the spy was a criminal.

Rudi had never meant to put his friend's family in danger. He got up to leave.

Sit down, the man gestured. "If you go out in the street on your own, you'll be picked up in five minutes," he said.

The man made a few phone calls, enlisted a few friends to help. They bought Rudi a train ticket to his next destination, the Hungarian capital of Budapest, and gave him a little money. They handed him an antisemitic newspaper to read on the train—good cover for a Jewish teen traveling without identity papers.

Rudi made it to Budapest. Friends from home had given him the address of a contact in the city, a member of an underground group that opposed Hungary's government and its alliance with Hitler. The man's brother let Rudi lay low for a few days, but warned him he'd never make it across Hungary without identity papers. False papers could be arranged, though it would take time. Rudi agreed to return to Slovakia, where it would be easier for him to hide, until the documents were ready.

Rudi took the night train back to Galanta and retraced his steps toward the fields along the frontier. He was pleased with himself. This was a retreat, but a temporary one—and look how much he'd seen and learned in just two weeks. He'd left home on his own, made new contacts, improved his plan.

"Halt!"

Rudi turned. There was just enough moonlight to make out the shapes of two soldiers, and the long barrels of their guns.

Rudi spun around and ran, struggling to gain speed in the slippery spring mud.

The soldiers started shooting.

Rudi stopped, panting.

The men marched toward him, rifles aimed at his chest.

This was a moment Rudi would think of often in the two-year nightmare to come. What if he hadn't stopped? Maybe one of those border guard's bullets would have taken him down.

Maybe not. It's tough to hit a moving target in the dark.

Anyway, he'd wish he had just kept running.

The Hungarian guards dragged Rudi to the nearest border station, and the interrogation began.

"Where are you going?"

"To Budapest," Rudi said.

One of the border guards punched him in the mouth, knocking him into the wall.

"Who do you know in Budapest?"

"Nobody."

They hit him again, this time with the butt of a gun.

Rudi fell to the floor, seeing sparks, tasting blood.

"You're a spy! Admit it!"

The beating continued—punch, question, punch—pausing only when an officer showed up. The older man looked through the scraps of paper the guards had pulled from Rudi's pockets.

"Where were you going?" the officer asked.

"To Budapest," Rudi said, straining to form words with swollen lips. "I'm a Slovak Jew. I didn't want to be deported. I've just crossed the border."

The officer unfolded a crumpled paper, one of the scraps from Rudi's pocket.

Rudi flinched when he saw it: a ticket from a Budapest tram. So much for just having crossed the border into Hungary.

"You're a spy," the officer charged. "Who are your accomplices?"

"I'm a refugee. I have no accomplices."

"You're a spy."

And the beating started up again. The questions and the blows.

"You're a spy. Who are your friends?"

Rudi wouldn't talk. It would have been so easy to give the address of the contact he'd met in Budapest. He wouldn't do it.

He was barely conscious when he heard the officer give his men new orders: "Take him back to the border. The usual treatment."

5

RUDI OPENED HIS EYES. HE was lying on cold mud. It was still night.

"Jesus, he's still alive," someone said—in Slovak.

Strong hands lifted Rudi. A man in a uniform, a Slovak border guard.

"You should be dead," the man said. "We always find them dead."

How long had he been out? Minutes? Hours? Rudi wasn't sure. Two young Hungarian guards had marched him into a field. They'd knocked him down, stuck a bayonet to his throat, but didn't have the heart to finish the job. They'd let him run for the border, and he'd sprinted for maybe a hundred yards before falling facedown in the mud and passing out.

Now two Slovak border guards guided Rudi to the local police station. They shoved him into a chair. There was no point in lying anymore. Rudi told them what he'd been trying to do.

"So you don't want to go to a resettlement area," said the guard who'd found him. "You don't want to work. You dirty, bloody Yid, I should beat you so your mother wouldn't recognize you. But that's been done already!"

They locked him in a cell. He collapsed onto the concrete plank that served for a bed. He was drifting off when he heard a voice, an old woman's voice.

"Mr. Jew . . . are you asleep?"

Rudi's body screamed with pain as he sat up. He looked to the small, barred window in the outer wall of the cell. A woman's hand reached through the bars. Food and cigarettes dropped to the cell floor.

Word of his arrest had spread, Rudi realized. Someone had taken pity on him. A kind gesture, but ominous also. He wasn't a teenager anymore, not to most of the people in what he'd thought was his country. He wasn't a kid who should be in high school, playing soccer and going to dances.

He was "Mr. Jew." Nothing more.

This was hardly new in Europe. More than fifteen centuries before, some early church leaders had begun speaking of Jews as outcasts, as people destined to suffer for sticking to their own religion rather than accepting Christianity. Kings reinforced this prejudice, issuing laws banning Jews from owning land, attending universities, or working in most professions.

Antisemitism, like other forms of prejudice and racism, has always been rooted in ignorance and lies. During the Middle Ages, Jewish communities faced a series of ridiculous charges: They murdered Christian children and used their blood in religious rituals, some said. They spread bubonic plague by poisoning wells. European rulers routinely expelled Jews, or segregated Jewish communities into impoverished "ghettos"—a term taken from a section of the Italian city of Venice into which Jewish homes were confined in the 1500s.

Early in the twentieth century, antisemitism took on a dangerous new element: the myth that Jews were somehow plotting to control the world. This conspiracy theory was sparked in large part by *The Protocols of the Elders of Zion*, a text that first appeared in Russia in 1903. The *Protocols* supposedly contained the minutes of secret meetings at which Jewish leaders made plans to manipulate the global economy and gain world domination.

Journalists exposed the text as a complete hoax. This fact did not stop the lies from spreading. Translations of the *Protocols* were published all over the world—including by Henry Ford, the famous American automaker, in his *Dearborn Independent* newspaper in the early 1920s.

Adolf Hitler endlessly echoed these debunked conspiracies. Did he worry that telling such obvious untruths would damage his credibility? Not at all. In his own book, *Mein Kampf,* Hitler wrote of the power of what he called a "big lie" to influence at least part of the public.

When the Office of Strategic Services, the American wartime intelligence agency, compiled a psychological profile of the German dictator, the authors noted Hitler's reliance on blatant lies. Among what the report called Hitler's "primary rules" was this: "People will believe a big lie sooner than a little one; and if you repeat it frequently enough people will sooner or later believe it."

Hitler's lies had terrible consequences for the Jewish population of Europe. To the old woman outside his jail cell, Rudi was "Mr. Jew."

To the authorities in Slovakia, Rudi was a little less than human and would be treated accordingly.

They dumped him in Nováky, a prison camp in central Slovakia.

Rudi was locked in a long barracks with hundreds of other prisoners. He could leave the building, under guard, only to use the latrine. The one thing he could figure out about Nováky was that it was a transit camp, a place to hold Jews slated for "resettlement."

Rudi approached prisoners who'd been in camp a while. What did they think the chances were of escape?

They laughed at him. The camp was surrounded by barbed wire, patrolled by armed Hlinka guards.

Rudi was not so easily discouraged. In his brief trips to the latrine, he noticed there was a second section of the prison, some sort of labor camp. The men over there worked in the sunshine, doing various construction jobs. It looked a lot nicer than the stuffy barracks.

Better yet, it might be possible to escape from that side of camp.

There had to be some way to get over there. Rudi kept his eyes open and found it. The guards used prisoners to carry food between the different sections of the camp. He volunteered for the task.

On his first trip to the labor camp, Rudi liked what he saw. Warm sun. Chirping birds. And long stretches of sagging barbed wire, with hundreds of yards between guards.

He nearly made a break for it right there. It was so tempting.

Go under the wire and head for the trees . . .

But he'd learned a few things about life on the run. He'd need extra clothing, at the very least. Some money would help. He decided to take a little time to prepare.

6

FOR GERTA'S FAMILY IN TRNAVA, the spring of 1942 was a time of family meetings, of hasty gatherings between her parents, aunts, and uncles. The town's young Jewish men were being resettled. How long until authorities came for the rest of them?

But what options did they have? Where could they go?

Gerta watched the adults spread out maps of the world, searching for a solution that did not exist.

More than two million European Jews had settled in the United States in the past few decades, but the American government had shut that door in the 1920s with strict immigration quotas. Since the start of the war, the U.S. Congress had considered several bills that would have let in more refugees from Nazi-dominated Europe. Anti-immigration members of the House and Senate, along with "America First" voices in the media, ensured that none passed. A proposal to admit twenty thousand refugee children was never even brought to a vote.

You couldn't get into Britain either, not without influential connections. And other countries made it clear that Jews were not welcome. As far as Gerta's parents could see, the only real hope was Hungary. Cross the border into Hungary and try to live there illegally, posing as Hungarian Christians.

"What will we do there?" Gerta's father wondered. "We will have no money, and we will not be able to work."

The family stayed home nearly all the time, laying low, hoping for a sudden change in the course of the war. Gerta, now fifteen, passed the time studying secretarial skills. She had zero interest in being a secretary. Like Rudi's study of Russian, practicing typing and shorthand was just something to do, something to occupy her gifted mind.

And as with Rudi's Russian, Gerta never could have dreamt how useful this knowledge was going to be.

At Nováky, Rudi continued delivering food to the labor camp. He spent a few weeks studying the prisoners, searching for someone who might help him escape. How could he know who to trust?

He couldn't. He'd just have to guess.

He liked the looks of a middle-aged plumber, a man with a kind face who sang while fixing pipes in the camp kitchen. Rudi took off his jacket and approached the man.

"Would you look after this for me until tomorrow?" Rudi asked. "It's too hot to wear it today."

Sure, the plumber said, he'd stash it in his tool locker.

The next day, Rudi brought an extra pair of socks. "Could you stow these for me somewhere?" he asked the plumber.

This would make his intention to escape obvious, Rudi knew. It was a huge risk.

The man stuffed the socks in his pocket and went on tinkering with a leaky faucet.

One item at a time, Rudi smuggled over everything from his travel bag, and then the bag itself.

Back in the barracks, he made friends with Josef Knapp, a boy his age from the town of Topol'čany, where Rudi was born. Josef had also been caught trying to get to Britain. He was eager to try again, and mentioned a rich father who'd gladly finance his illegal travels. Rudi told Josef he was going to escape in a few days. He invited Josef to come along.

Rudi persuaded the guards that he needed Josef to help him carry food around the labor camp. Everything was set.

Rudi led his friend into the labor camp kitchen. The plumber was there, working at a sink. One look at Rudi and Josef and he understood. There was a guard in the kitchen, but he seemed busy grazing on the food lying around.

The plumber hurried to his barracks. He came out with Rudi's loaded pack.

"God bless you," he said, shoving some coins into Rudi's hand, then turning quickly away.

Rudi and Josef walked along the barbed wire. No guards in sight.

They dove under the wire, skidded down a steep hill, splashed across a shallow stream, and charged into the woods, laughing like kids with the joy of running free.

The teens slept in a cornfield, woken once by the wail of a distant train. They wondered where the train was going. They were glad not to be on it.

The friends were on the move again before dawn. The plan was to head for Topoľčany, about twenty-five miles from the Nováky prison camp. Josef was a familiar face in town; he couldn't just stroll in unnoticed. But Rudi's family had moved away when he was a few years old. No one knew him there. The idea was that Rudi would slip in and find the house where Josef's girlfriend, Zuzka, lived with her parents. He'd tell Zuzka where Josef was hiding, and she'd go to him. Then Josef would figure out a way to get Rudi some cash, and Rudi could continue his journey from there.

Rudi knocked on Zuzka's door at nine in the morning. The girl showed him in and listened to his story with growing excitement. She hadn't heard from her boyfriend since he'd left for Britain. She was amazed to hear he was so close.

"I must go to him at once," she said. "Momma will look after you until I get back."

And she dashed out the door.

Rudi was left with the parents. Nice-seeming folks who weren't quite clear on who this boy was or why he was in their parlor.

The father smiled at Rudi with more embarrassment than warmth. "It's a little difficult right now," he began. "You see, they're rounding up the . . . Jews."

So this was not a Jewish home, Rudi realized. He was a danger to them, just by being there.

The parents suggested he hide in their shed until Zuzka returned, and Rudi jumped at the offer. The mother brought him food. Not a bad setup, much better than Nováky.

But where was Zuzka? Where was the money Josef had promised?

Hours passed. Then a whole afternoon, and a long night. Rudi spent the first half of the next day in the shed, nervousness giving way to fury. Where the hell was Josef? How could his friend just abandon him like that?

And here was the father again, with that same pathetic grin. "It's all very difficult," he said, "but she hasn't come back."

Rudi got the message. Time to move on.

He needed to get back to Trnava. With any luck, the contact he'd met in Hungary had sent the forged identity papers he'd promised. Rudi could walk home in a few days—if his shoes held out. They weren't made for long hikes across the country and were coming apart.

Figuring he'd blend in better without his bag, Rudi left it in the shed. He pulled on a second pair of socks. It was too hot for extra socks, but at least this way he'd have them for later. He hadn't forgotten his mother's parting advice: "Don't forget to change your socks."

He laced up what was left of his shoes and headed into town.

7

THE BUILDINGS AND STREETS OF Topoľčany looked vaguely familiar to Rudi. He stopped outside one house, struck by an odd sight: furniture in the front garden. Not stacked up for a move, but spread out, as if on display. Rudi could guess what this meant.

He knocked on the door and spoke with the homeowner, a middle-aged man. Yes, the man said, he and his family were Jewish. The family was being moved by order of the government. Resettled. Local authorities would sell the furniture, and no doubt pocket the cash.

This was news to Rudi. It was not just young men anymore. Now entire families were being taken away.

It felt awkward to ask this man for anything. But where else could he turn for help? Rudi managed to get out the words, "If you had an old pair of shoes . . ."

The man turned and walked into his house. He came back with a pair of brown leather shoes.

"They belong to my son," the man said. "He went two months ago."

The shoes fit and were practically new. A lucky break. Rudi couldn't help but wonder where the man's son was right now . . . but still, he was feeling a bit better about his chances of making it back to Trnava.

Ducking into a little food shop, he drank a glass of milk at the counter. A policeman strolled in and stood beside him, looking him over. Rudi glanced at the revolver in the man's holster, then up at his face. They exchanged friendly nods. Rudi drained his glass and left.

He was walking down the street, trying not to hurry, when he heard the sound of a bicycle behind him. Wheels skidding to a stop.

The police officer from the café sat on his bike, one foot on the sidewalk. Not smiling anymore. "Good afternoon. May I see your documents, please?"

Rudi froze, thinking of the beating he'd taken from those border guards in Hungary. Thinking of the whistle of trains in the night.

He let out a scream and ran.

Rudi tore down the city street and circled a busy newspaper kiosk like a mouse in a cartoon. The policeman grabbed for him, swerving his bicycle to avoid obstacles, sliding around on the pavement. People stopped to watch; some even cheered. Dodging through the crowd, Rudi sprinted down a side street he hoped would lead out of town.

It was a dead end. He stopped and turned.

The policeman rode up, streaming sweat. He stepped off his bike, let it fall, and asked, "Are you a Jew or a thief?"

What other reason would the boy have for running from the law?

"A Jew," Rudi said.

They looked at each other, both trying to catch their breath. Rudi saw sympathy in the man's eyes. But he could hardly hope to go free, not after half the town had seen the chase.

The man marched Rudi toward the police station. "Do you know why I asked for your documents?"

Rudi didn't.

"I saw you were wearing two pairs of socks," the policeman explained. "Two pairs of socks in this weather!"

Another valuable lesson. Wearing two pairs of socks in June makes it look like you're on the run.

He'd remember that for next time.

Back in Trnava, time ran out for Gerta.

She was practicing her typing late one night when the doorbell rang. She opened the door. It was a friend of her father's, clearly upset.

"Please tell your father that I need to talk to him," he said.

He was asleep, Gerta told the man. Couldn't it wait?

It couldn't. "Go and wake him."

Her father, Max, came out of his bedroom. He and his friend went into the living room to talk in private.

Gerta sat outside the room, looking at the furniture, the photos on the walls, a porcelain figurine of a shepherd playing a flute. None of this stuff really mattered, she knew. But she had a feeling she'd never see any of it again. She wanted the pictures in her memory.

Her father came out of the living room, slouched over and pale.

"We have to leave the house tonight," he told Gerta. The

authorities would be rounding up the remaining Jews in Trnava in the morning. "No one seems to know where the Jews are being sent to," he said, "but it is better not to be included in the transport."

Gerta dressed in dark clothes. She tied a black scarf over her fair hair. She packed a spare outfit, a toothbrush, and a comb. She and her mother, Jozefina, would set out first, the family decided. Max would travel separately, hopefully giving them all a better chance to evade notice.

Gerta and Jozefina took a taxi to a village along the border. Relatives arranged for a young man to meet them there and guide them across the dark fields to Hungary. They hiked through the night and reached a small Hungarian town just before dawn. The guide slipped away before the women could even thank him.

Roosters crowed in yards around the village. A church bell clanged. Two Hungarian border guards patrolled the road up ahead. Gerta took her mother's arm and led her into the church.

Their only chance was to blend in. Gerta thought back to the few times she'd been to mass with Catholic friends. She remembered something about touching the water in the bowl at the entrance and making the sign of the cross with her hand. Her mother followed her lead.

"I felt in every fiber of my body that the fight for survival had started in earnest," Gerta would later say. "I was determined to do my best to win."

8

AFTER A FEW DAYS UNDER close guard at the Nováky prison camp, Rudi marched with a group of prisoners to a waiting train. Soldiers with guns surrounded the station.

"Try to escape again," one of them warned Rudi, "and you're a dead duck."

They shoved him into a boxcar with at least eighty other people and their luggage. The doors slammed. A lock clicked shut. The train jerked forward and rattled out of the station.

Rudi could see a bit of the passing landscape through the bars of a tiny window. They were heading northeast. Toward Poland. Resettlement. Exactly what he'd been trying so hard to avoid.

The car was so packed that only a few people could sit down at once. There was a mix of young and old, women and men. That was one sliver of mercy—Slovakia's president, Jozef Tiso, had promised that families could stay together. People seemed in decent spirits, Rudi thought. They talked of everyday things. Had they remembered to turn off the gas? To cancel the milk delivery? It was as if they still hadn't accepted that any of this was real.

Rudi spotted a friend of his from home, Tomasov, with a teenage girl he didn't recognize. They saw Rudi and wriggled toward him.

"Your sister?" Rudi asked.

"My wife," Tomasov proudly announced. They'd married two weeks ago so that they could stay together when they were resettled.

Word spread that there were newlyweds aboard. People cheered the couple and passed over small offerings from the food they'd brought along for the journey.

The conversation turned to what came next. Where were they going? What would the resettlement area be like?

Most people seemed to expect some sort of labor camp or ghetto. Maybe it wouldn't be too awful, and they could return home when the war was over.

A young girl asked her father: Would there be schools? Playgrounds?

The father told his daughter what she needed to hear. Yes, he said. Schools and playgrounds.

A girl of about sixteen said she'd recently gotten a letter from a cousin, someone who'd been resettled with an earlier group. Everything was fine, the cousin reported. Enough food, and the work wasn't too hard. "There was only one thing I couldn't understand," the girl said. "She said her mother sent me her love. And her mother died three years ago."

Another woman, a mother holding a baby, told a similar story.

She'd gotten a letter from her sister, who'd been resettled, and the sister wrote that a friend of theirs, Jakob Rakow, was doing well.

The strange thing was that Jakob Rakow had died in a car accident years before.

Had these people been forced to write letters to their families saying everything was fine? Had they slipped in details their relatives would recognize as wrong as some sort of warning?

"You're fools if you think you're going to resettlement areas," one young man told the group. "We're all going to die!"

Rudi didn't believe it. No one in the car believed it.

In fact, the killing had already begun. The Nazis' attempt to murder the entire Jewish population of Europe—Adolf Hitler's "Final Solution"—had already begun.

As German forces drove hundreds of miles into the Soviet Union, Nazi police and SS units known as Einsatzgruppen—special action groups—traveled behind the advancing army. Their task was to round up Jewish people in occupied towns and shoot them. The Einsatzgruppen murdered six hundred thousand men, women, and children in 1941, and the killing continued into 1942. Secret reports on the mass shootings, with photographs, were sent to Hitler in Berlin.

The killings were too big to hide entirely. Allied intelligence agents inside Europe began hearing stories of the murders. Small numbers of people who were able to escape occupied territory and reach Britain, or neutral countries such as Switzerland, told of what they'd seen and heard. Newspapers in Britain and the United States reported briefly on stories of mass killings—but treated these stories as unverified rumors. The great battles raging in Europe and Asia dominated the news.

At the Auschwitz concentration camp in southern Poland, Kommandant Rudolf Höss thought about what SS chief Heinrich Himmler had told him: "Now, during the war, all the Jews we can lay hands on are to be exterminated, without exception."

Höss did not like the idea of mass shootings at Auschwitz. He was worried not about the victims but about the emotional impact on his staff. "To remove the anticipated multitudes by shooting would be absolutely impossible," he'd later explain, "and, in respect of the women and children, would impose too great a strain on the SS men who would have to carry it out."

Höss decided to use poison gas. There was precedent for this. With Hitler's approval, the Nazis had already used poison gas to murder tens of thousands of Germans with mental illnesses or physical disabilities.

In September 1941, the Auschwitz staff tested their first gas chamber. Guards forced Soviet prisoners of war into a basement room in Block 11, the camp's punishment block. They threw in Zyklon B—toxic hydrogen cyanide in crystal form, a pesticide used in camp to kill vermin and disinfect clothes.

The prisoners all died, but Höss was not satisfied. The basement room had no ventilation, so it had to be aired out a long time before the bodies could be removed. Also, Block 11 was across camp from the crematorium building, where the bodies of dead prisoners were burned. Hauling wagons of corpses across camp, Höss feared, could cause unnecessary panic among the prisoners.

The kommandant's solution was to build a gas chamber inside

the crematorium building. A morgue room, which already had a ventilation system, was equipped with airtight doors. Holes were drilled in the roof so that poison could be dropped in from above.

Höss stood outside his new gas chamber as nine hundred Soviet prisoners were locked inside. Guards dropped in Zyklon B. The green-blue crystals went directly from solid to deadly gas in the warm air of the crowded room. Höss, wearing a gas mask for safety, listened to the men scream and bang on the door, and then go silent.

"I must admit openly that the gassings had a calming effect on me," he would later say, "since in the near future the mass annihilation of the Jews was to begin."

The Nazis began killing Jewish prisoners in the Auschwitz gas chamber in the spring of 1942. Just as Rudi Vrba was swept into Hitler's complex of concentration camps.

9

RUDI'S TRAIN CROSSED INTO POLAND and rolled slowly north, pulling several times onto sidetracks to make way for German military trains. Rudi stuck by the window, trying to follow the route, straining to remember a geography class in which they'd studied this part of Europe.

A full day passed, and a full night. The doors never opened, even when the train was stopped. The wagon baked in the sun. Nearly everyone had been standing for more than twenty-four hours. There was one bucket in the corner to use as a toilet, and the stench of waste filled the hot air. Children begged parents for water, which had long since run out.

By the second day in the train, terrible thirst overtook the other miseries, even the fear of where they were going. It was torture to Rudi to look out at streams winding their way beside the tracks.

The train finally stopped. The doors slid open. Black-uniformed soldiers of the SS patrolled the yard.

"One man out to get water," an SS man shouted into Rudi's car. "Nobody else must move!"

A man near the door jumped out and lined up with people from the other cars. He was nearly to the water pump when a soldier ordered everyone back on the train.

"I haven't filled my can yet," the man said.

An SS man smacked him with the butt of his gun and shoved him back into the boxcar. The doors slid shut. The padlock clicked. The car was absolutely silent.

The train continued, heading east now. Rudi watched what had been a sort of community in the wagon break down into small groups, with adults looking out for their young children and elderly parents.

Hours later they stopped again. The doors opened. They were in the city of Lublin.

Soldiers surrounded the train, some with submachine guns, some with horse whips and bamboo canes.

An SS officer shouted: "All men between sixteen and forty-five out!"

It was a mistake. That was Rudi's first thought. It had to be a mistake.

Others were clearly thinking the same. President Tiso had promised that families would stay together. No one got off the train.

"Come on!" the SS men roared. "You heard!"

Rudi and the other young men still hesitated—still thinking they lived in a world with rules.

"All men between sixteen and forty-five out! The rest stay where they are!"

One by one, the men jumped to the ground. Soldiers slammed the wagon doors shut.

"My wife's in there!" Rudi's friend Tomasov cried. "Let her out!"

An SS man whipped him in the face, cutting open his cheek.

As the train began to move, women, children, and grandparents reached hands out between bars and through the narrow gap between the chained wagon doors. Nazi guards swung their canes and whips, forcing the hands back in.

The train rolled out of the yard and was gone. It had all happened so fast.

Rudi saw shock on the other men's faces. Agony.

The SS lined the men up and marched them off at a fast pace. Rudi stole a look at the trees along the side of the road. Was there a chance to make a run for it?

Someone tried it, a man in front of Rudi. The SS shot him dead before he was off the road.

They marched through the back streets of Lublin and out toward a prison camp. Rows of barracks were surrounded by barbed wire and tall watchtowers. Guards opened the gates of the camp as the group approached.

Rudi had been hearing about Hitler's concentration camps for years, though he knew nothing of the camps the Nazis had built in Poland since the start of the war. He had no idea what to expect at this camp, Majdanek.

The first impression was shocking.

As his group marched in, Rudi saw windowless wooden barracks in a field of mud. Emaciated men with shaved heads, wearing striped prisoner uniforms, moved around pushing wheelbarrows, digging holes. They were closely watched by healthier-looking men in a strange assortment of mismatched clothing, with green triangles sewn on their shirts. These men carried clubs and swung them at prisoners to hurry them along.

"Any food?" prisoners whispered as they passed the new arrivals, never looking up. "Any food?"

Rudi's group was marched through the camp. He kept seeing people he recognized, people from Trnava, teachers, shopkeepers. He saw a friend from school, Erwin Eisler, pushing a wheelbarrow.

Erwin, the brave boy who'd secretly kept his chemistry textbook. He was just seventeen, like Rudi, but stooped over now, half the weight he'd been back home. Erwin noticed his friend staring and moved closer, eyes on the ground.

"How is it here?" Rudi asked.

Erwin looked at Rudi, hesitating, as if trying to think of some gentle way to put it. His face told the story, the bones almost sticking through the skin. He asked Rudi for food. Rudi had none.

Erwin attempted a smile. He gripped the handles of his wheelbarrow and walked away.

They'd been told families would stay together. That was a lie. They'd been told they were going to be put to work. But what was the work? Moving dirt around a prison camp? What was the point of this place?

Rudi got no answers, not right away. His group washed with cold water and had their heads shaved. They got striped prisoner outfits and wooden clogs for their feet.

Rudi picked up the camp routine over the next few days: lining up outside his barracks for morning roll call, removing his cap and looking down when an SS man walked by. He was put to work carrying bricks and lumber from one part of camp to another. Materials for expanding the camp, he figured.

The men with the mismatched clothing, he learned, were known as kapos—non-Jewish prisoners with authority in camp. The green triangles meant they were career criminals. Other kapos wore red triangles, indicating they were political prisoners.

Kapos supervised the work of Jewish prisoners with a mixture of shouts and beatings. When Rudi made the mistake of speaking to another prisoner within earshot of a kapo, the man bashed Rudi with a club. Working slowly would get you a beating. Crying out while being beaten would get you a longer beating.

For food they got thin soup and stale chunks of bread. *How long can you live on that?* Rudi wondered.

Every night prisoners in Rudi's barracks died from starvation or disease. It was the job of the living to carry the bodies to roll call in the morning.

One day, while working, Rudi saw a prisoner make a sudden dash for the camp's outer ring of barbed wire. The SS guards shot him before he got close. Did the man really think he could get through? Or did he just want to end it quickly? Either way, there was no getting out like that. Not alive.

This was worth knowing. Because the more Rudi saw of Majdanek, the more determined he was to escape.

10

GERTA WAS CONFINED TO A very different kind of prison: a tiny apartment in Budapest, Hungary.

Her father, Max, had made it safely across the border, and relatives in Hungary helped the family get forged identity papers. Posing as a Catholic family from the countryside, they'd rented a small flat in the city.

But Gerta and her parents were still far from safe. Anyone could be a police informant, including the concierge who lived on the ground floor and kept a nosy watch on the building's residents. Perhaps he was already wondering why the new teenage tenant never left for school or work.

Gerta's first task was to memorize facts about the Hungarian village she supposedly came from. That was fairly easy. The real issue was the Hungarian language. She spoke well enough to get by, but with a Slovak accent that would instantly expose her as an immigrant.

Her mother saw that she was brooding, bored and lonely, worried sick about her friends. Jozefina sent her daughter out on a simple errand: buy some matches.

Gerta pointed out the accent problem.

"I know," Jozefina said, "but you have to learn fast, and this is the way to do it."

Accepting the challenge, Gerta walked to the nearest shop. Non-Jewish adults had often told her she did not "look Jewish"—disturbingly, they meant it as a compliment. But could her fair hair and blue eyes be an asset now?

Gerta entered the store—and promptly blanked on the Hungarian word for matches.

"Only the Slovak and German words kept popping into my memory," she'd recall. "I was terribly embarrassed and walked out of the shop."

Frightened but determined, Gerta practiced a bit more with her mother. She walked to a different shop, asked for a box of matches, paid, and walked home.

Such a small thing. But it was a turning point for Gerta. She spent the next six weeks repeating Hungarian phrases over and over, slowly improving her pronunciation. "Gradually," she'd say, "I became quite expert in impersonating a Hungarian country girl."

From now on, she understood, deception would be essential to her chances of survival.

A few days after arriving at Majdanek, Rudi was stacking a pile of lumber when he noticed a kapo standing nearby, watching. Rudi piled the wood a bit faster, hoping to avoid a blow from the man's cane.

The kapo stepped closer. "Come with me," he said in Czech. "I've a job for you."

They walked across the muddy yard and stopped in front of what was, in this place, a beautiful sight: an enormous pile of potatoes.

The kapo ordered Rudi to carry a load of potatoes into the kitchen. He smacked Rudi on the back, told him to hurry. Rudi couldn't believe his luck. Kitchen jobs were coveted in camp—for the opportunity to steal food. He was able to snatch a few cooked potatoes that afternoon. By concentration camp standards, a feast.

And there was more good news. That night, after roll call, one of the kapos asked the prisoners if any of them knew anything about farm work. "We're sending four hundred men to a farm," the kapo announced.

Rudi volunteered. About a thousand people stepped forward, eager to get out any way they could. Rudi was among those chosen, probably because he was so young and because he'd been in camp less than two weeks. His body had not yet begun to break down.

The next morning, the Czech kapo again put Rudi to work lugging potatoes. The kapo, a man named Milan, seemed to be a decent guy. He only caned Rudi when the SS guards were watching, and never with much force. He even offered to get Rudi assigned to kitchen duty full-time.

Rudi was thankful, but said he'd be leaving soon. He explained about volunteering for farm work. The train was leaving in a few days.

"Are you crazy?" Milan asked. "Do you know where that train's going?"

Rudi admitted he didn't. He was already picturing himself under the sun in a giant field of wheat. A field was a lot harder to guard than a prison camp. There might be a chance to get away. Even the train ride might offer an opportunity to escape. And from what Rudi could see, no one was going to live very long at Majdanek.

He told Milan, "Anywhere's better than this dump."

The four hundred farm volunteers were given civilian clothes— to avoid drawing attention as they traveled? That was Rudi's guess. Flanked by SS men, they marched in a column out of Majdanek. Rudi felt lucky to be leaving while still healthy and strong.

"You will be given food for the journey," a Nazi officer told the group at the train station in Lublin. "Save this food, for I have no idea how long we will be traveling. And remember—it is useless trying to escape."

They each got some bread with marmalade and a hunk of salami. Rudi crowded into one of the boxcars with about eighty other men. The doors closed and the train left the station, heading west.

Rudi began pondering escape options. He looked around the car, hoping to find an accomplice, and spotted the blond hair and lanky frame of Josef Erdelyi. They'd been in the Nováky camp together back in Slovakia, and were the same age.

Rudi shoved his way to Josef. They had a whispered conversation. Josef was in.

The friends studied the cramped space. The tiny window was barred. The door was chained shut. What about the weathered wooden floor? Could they crack a few boards and slip out? They agreed to assess their chances at the first stop.

Late that night the train slowed down. They rolled through a town and stopped on a dark stretch of track just beyond the station. The doors opened.

Dozens of SS guards, with their submachine guns, had already formed a cordon around the train.

Rudi looked to Josef. They both had the same thought: *Not a chance.*

As if reading their minds, an SS officer announced that the prisoners would be counted here, and several more times along the way. "If at any stage any man is missing," the officer warned, "ten men in his wagon will be shot."

That was it. Rudi gave up on escaping from the train.

"Don't worry," Josef whispered. "There's still the farm ahead of us."

The train continued west for two more days and nights. The food ran out. The bucket overflowed with filth. As before, the worst torment was thirst.

They stopped on the night of June 30. The SS formed the men into columns, and they marched along a road, their ridiculous wooden clogs click-clacking on the pavement. The road led toward a large camp, lit up by a ring of searchlights on watchtowers. They passed through the front gates, beneath a steel archway with the German words ARBEIT MACHT FREI—*Work makes one free.*

So they were here to work? Rudi was not afraid of work. As they lined up for yet another count, Rudi's eyes darted around, taking in images:

Rows of two-story brick buildings, orderly looking and clean compared to Majdanek.

Armed SS men all around, many holding big German shepherds on leashes.

Searchlights on watchtowers, and guards with guns gazing down.

Concrete posts, maybe twelve feet high, strung top to bottom with rows of electrified barbed wire, penning in the whole camp.

Why in the world is there so much security?

Some of the prisoners managed a bitter laugh, whispering jokes about how frightening they must be to these poor Nazis.

It wasn't fear, Rudi sensed. It was something else. Something he did not yet understand.

The men were marched into one of the brick buildings and down a set of stairs to the basement. They passed a water tap on the wall but were not permitted to drink. Several kapos thumped down the stairs in heavy boots and stood in front of the newcomers.

One of the kapos, a thickset man in striped prisoner pants and a blue jacket, wearing the green triangle of a career criminal, stepped forward.

"I am the block senior here," he began. "You're in Auschwitz concentration camp, and you'd better not forget it."

Anyone leaving the barracks at night would be shot, he warned. Anyone drinking water from that tap, he said, pointing to the wall, would get dysentery. A death sentence in this place.

"Drink only tea," he told them. "You'll get it in the morning. And remember—here are only the healthy or the dead."

The kapo turned and climbed the stairs, his lackeys close behind.

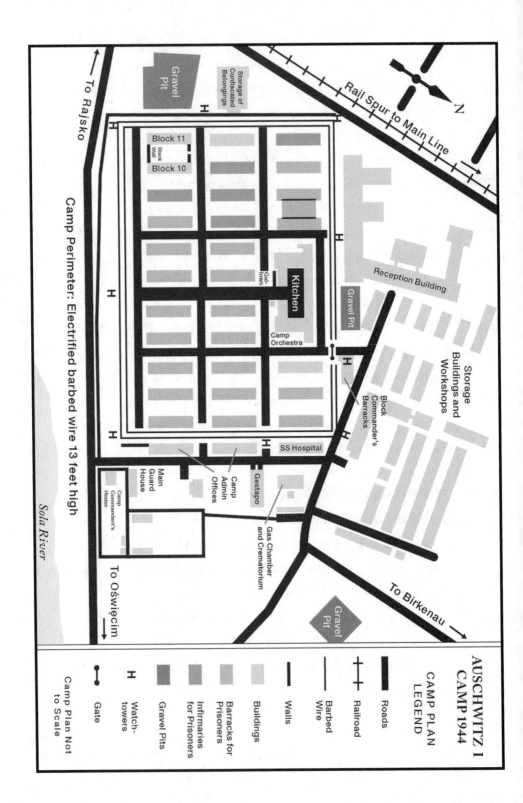

11

"I AM ENTIRELY NORMAL," RUDOLF Höss would tell an American psychologist after the war. "Even while I was doing the extermination work, I led a normal family life."

Soon after taking over at Auschwitz, Höss had moved with his wife, Hedwig, and their four children into a riverside villa on the edge of camp. The property featured gardens and a greenhouse, and room for the kids to run around and ride bicycles. In the living room hung photos of the children sitting on the lap of Heinrich Himmler—Uncle Heiner, as they called him—taken on one of Himmler's recent inspection visits.

From the window of his second-story bedroom, Höss could see the tall brick chimney of the Auschwitz crematorium. But while at home, he'd later explain, he tried not to think of such unpleasant things.

He never spoke to his wife of the true purpose of Auschwitz, though of course the family knew they were living at a prison camp. Höss brought in prisoners to take care of the house and grounds, even to cut his hair. The barber job was given to a young Polish free-dom fighter, Józef Paczyński, who would never forget the first time he was ordered to follow Hedwig up the stairs to a small bathroom. The kommandant came in without saying a word, sat on a chair, lit a cigar, and started flipping through a newspaper.

Józef's hands began shaking. "I had a razor in my hand," he'd later recall. "I could have cut his throat—it could have happened. But I'm a thinking being, and you know what would have happened? My whole family would have been destroyed; half the camp would be destroyed. In his place someone else would have come."

Was there *any* effective way to fight back against such over-whelming evil?

So many prisoners—including Rudi Vrba—would wrestle with this seemingly unanswerable question.

A loud bell woke the camp at 5:00 a.m. Rudi watched prisoners carry in barrels of steaming liquid. He was served a portion and gulped it down. This, evidently, was the "tea"—gray and bitter. Rudi wished he could have more.

Then Rudi's group of new arrivals filed outside for roll call and were told they'd not yet been assigned to work details. What were they supposed to do? No one said. Rudi decided to walk around a little, look around if no one stopped him.

A man from the train walked alongside him, saying, "Maybe I'll find my son here."

Maybe, Rudi agreed.

The man, Ipi Müller, was about Rudi's mother's age. He'd spent half the train trip telling people about his son Filip, a talented young violinist. It was moving, Rudi thought, the way just saying Filip's name gave Ipi joy, transported some part of him out of the filthy wagon.

Suddenly, they heard music. Not a recording. Live musicians playing a military march. Rudi turned around and saw, far off by the front gates, prisoners playing violins and cellos and horns. A conductor waving his baton.

An orchestra? In this diabolical place?

Ipi grabbed Rudi's arm. "He'll be there, Rudi. He'll be up there, playing."

But they couldn't get close enough to look for Filip among the musicians. Kapos began shouting to large groups of prisoners:

"To work!"

"To work!"

Thousands of prisoners marched out through the front gates. Kommandant Höss inspected the parade, hollering over and over, "Work makes life sweet!"

This procession looked to Rudi like a ghoulish hallucination. A military-style march in rows of five, neat and orderly—but when you focused in on individual people you could see that many of them were skeletal and wobbling.

Still, those men got to leave camp. That was something. Wherever they were going couldn't be as heavily guarded as Auschwitz, Rudi figured.

The next morning, after roll call, Rudi's group was marched to a different building and ordered to undress.

"Into the showers!"

The kapos drove the prisoners into a small washroom for a quick, freezing rinse.

"Out! Everybody out! Faster, swine!"

Dodging the kapos' clubs and boots, Rudi stumbled naked into the morning sun. He joined a line in front of a couple of small tables. At one table each prisoner was given a number. Rudi's number was 44070.

Forget your name, a kapo told them. You're a number now.

At the next table, a seated prisoner tattooed 44070 on Rudi's left forearm.

Finally, they were given clothes: striped pajamas and a floppy cap. Rudi was relieved to put something on.

They were marched to a new barracks and up the stairs to the attic. They got half a pint of tea and a piece of dusty bread, maybe two ounces.

Was there any chance, Rudi wondered, they were really going to be put to work on a farm?

A kapo walked in with a cane in his hand. The attic went silent.

The man looked well fed and strong. He had a red triangle on his shirt—a political prisoner. Was that a good sign? Not a murderer, at least? He seemed almost to be smiling, as if amused by the scene.

"Let's have a look at you bastards!" he shouted in German.

He strolled in front of the group, looking each man over, poking a few with the end of his cane. He raised the stick over one prisoner's head and the man tripped backward. The kapo chuckled and continued down the line.

He came to Rudi. Looked him up and down.

Rudi made up his mind to stand his ground, no matter what. He would not be laughed at.

The kapo made a fist and jabbed it into Rudi's gut. It hurt, but felt more like a test than an effort to injure. Rudi didn't budge.

"Strong boy, eh?" The kapo put a heavy hand on Rudi's arm and squeezed the muscle. "Speak German?"

"Fluently," Rudi said.

"You'll do."

Rudi later found out that the man, an Austrian named Franz, had bought him for one lemon.

Franz selected two other recruits from Rudi's train from Majdanek—Ipi Müller and Rudi's teenage friend, Josef Erdelyi.

"You're lucky boys to be taken off that agricultural work," Franz told them as he led them out of the barracks. "You know what it means? It means digging up bodies and burning them."

The bodies were those of prisoners murdered at Auschwitz, including thousands of Soviet prisoners of war. They'd been buried in mass graves, but camp authorities had now decided to burn the corpses to destroy evidence of their crimes. Rudi would learn these details later. For now, he only knew he'd been absurdly naïve. To have imagined himself in a wheat field, awaiting the right moment to make a break for the woods! It was the fantasy of a child.

Franz led the three prisoners down a road between rows of brick barracks. Whenever they passed SS guards, the kapo cursed his prisoners, "Jewish pigs" and so on, and swung his cane. But the stick barely touched them. It was just for show, Rudi realized.

Franz brought them into another barracks, a narrow, barnlike space with wooden rafters and tall rows of bunk beds, three levels high. Men lay in the bunks, or sat on the edges, three or four people in each tiny space. Rudi and Josef were surprised to get a bunk for just the two of them.

Rudi had no idea what sort of work Franz had picked him for, but sensed he'd finally gotten a bit of luck. That night he slept pretty well.

12

EARLY THE NEXT MORNING, FRANZ led his prisoners out the main gate, past the screeching Rudolf Höss—"Work makes life sweet!"—and along a road lined with buildings and trees.

The sight of green leaves was a small pleasure. The morning sun was warm. There were no SS guards in sight. Rudi and Josef shared a quick smile. Both were thinking the same thing:

We've just found the easy way out of Auschwitz!

They came to a large building alongside a railroad line. Franz led the group inside some kind of warehouse. Rudi had been in concentration camps for about two months, long enough to completely alter the way he thought about food. Long enough to be shocked by the sight of crates of canned ham and beef, jars of jam and fruit, cases of sparkling water, piled high in stacks the size of houses.

"This is the SS food store," Franz explained to the new men in his crew. "Your job will be to unload the railway wagons outside and to stack the stuff neatly here."

He showed the men where to wash up with soap and towels, another luxury.

"Now get to work, you lazy brutes."

A train rolled up and stopped in front of the building. Rudi and Josef were both laughing as they ran outside. Each grabbed a few cases of Hungarian pickles and carried them inside. Franz ordered them to stack the pickles in a third-floor storage room. Rudi could hear Josef whistling behind him as they clopped up the stairs.

Rudi stole a moment to look out the storage room window. The view was a thing of beauty: a winding road, trees and more trees. So many places to hide. He lifted his eyes to take in a wider view of the landscape, and—

"Josef," Rudi said, suddenly deflated. "Come here."

Josef was still whistling, right up to the moment he stepped to the window.

"The bastards!"

They were not outside Auschwitz at all.

They'd marched out the main gate, yes, but that was only the inner perimeter of protection. From the storeroom they could see a second, much larger ring of fences and watchtowers. They could just make out guards in the distant towers, and their mounted machine guns, and more SS men patrolling the open space in front of the wire.

No one could cross that space without being seen—and shot.

Rudi and Josef went back to stacking crates.

As the weather warmed that spring, Gerta remained stuck in her family's apartment in Budapest. She set herself the challenge of reading novels and poetry in Hungarian, but the language came easily to her; it was not an effective distraction. "Often my thoughts were far away," she'd later say, "trying to join my old friends, imagining where they might be."

Most had left with their families—resettled, but where? And what about Rudi? Had he made it all the way to Britain? What was he doing now?

Gerta had no way to know. She knew she wouldn't hear from him anytime soon. If ever.

The strange thing—surreal to Gerta—was that no one else seemed worried.

Newspapers were filled with stories of epic battles between Axis and Allied forces in the Soviet Union and North Africa, in the Atlantic and Pacific Oceans. Yet people in Budapest didn't seem to think the war would affect them. The country's economy was booming. The shops were full, the movie theaters and restaurants bustling.

Even Gerta's Hungarian relatives felt safe. They were among Hungary's more than eight hundred thousand Jews—almost 9 percent of the country's population—and well assimilated into Hungarian life. Yes, the government had passed laws banning Jews from public office and limiting the number of Jews that could work in any given company. But to Gerta's relatives, Hungary was home. They were contributing to their country's success. Why would Hungary's leaders take the drastic step of forcing Jews to resettle elsewhere?

These points gave Gerta no comfort. She'd felt just as much at home in Slovakia as her relatives did in Hungary, just as much a part of the country. And look how quickly that had ended.

Seeing how lonely and depressed Gerta was, one of her Hungarian aunts arranged for her to meet two Jewish boys her own age.

Gerta walked to her aunt's apartment, looking forward to the gathering. But it was disappointing. Disturbing, even.

The boys babbled on about sports, about friends at school. Normal things—that's what was so unsettling. They seemed utterly uninterested in the war or the fate of Jewish people in countries under Nazi control. Such troubles, they seemed to think, would never touch their comfortable lives in Budapest.

"They never asked about me," Gerta recalled, "what it felt like being a refugee, assuming another identity, not being able to go to school."

The experience only made Gerta feel more alone. More anxious about the future.

In June 1942, Adolf Hitler secretly began pressuring his Hungarian allies to cooperate with the Nazis' "Final Solution."

Through the spring of 1942 and into the summer, Franz marched his crew out to the warehouse each morning and back through the main gates of Auschwitz each night. Once the prisoners were inside the camp's inner perimeter, they lined up for another count.

Rudi couldn't figure out why the Nazis were guarding them so closely. Normally you'd guard something valuable. But Auschwitz authorities obviously didn't value their prisoners—or they wouldn't beat and starve them to death. And yet the SS officers who ran the camp were clearly obsessed with crushing any hope of escape.

It made no sense to Rudi. Not yet.

After work one evening, there was a change in routine. Rudi lined up with thousands of other prisoners in a courtyard outside the camp kitchen. Two wooden gallows sat in front of the building. A row of SS guards, guns on straps over their shoulders, beat on military drums. Kommandant Höss looked on.

Another SS officer, one Rudi had seen being particularly vicious with prisoners, stepped forward. The drumming stopped.

"Two Polish prisoners have been caught preparing to escape," the officer shouted. The evidence? They'd been found with civilian shirts beneath their prisoner outfits. "Let it be a warning to you all!"

The drums started up again, a thunderous pounding. Two very thin prisoners marched up barefoot, hands tied behind their backs. Each climbed onto one of the platforms. A kapo, acting as the hangman, looped nooses around their necks. One of the prisoners shouted something—some burst of defiance, judging by the expression on his face—but Rudi couldn't hear his words over the drumming.

The kapo pulled a lever. The first prisoner fell through a trap door. Another lever, and the second man fell.

"Nobody moves!" roared the SS officer. "You stand there for an hour."

Rudi stood, forced to watch the two men suffocate.

The sun set. The lights in the watchtowers came on.

When he was finally permitted to move, Rudi walked past the bodies of the Polish prisoners. He noticed scraps of paper pinned to their shirts.

On each was written "Because we tried to escape."

Rudi thought: *When I get out of here and tell people about this place, no one's going to believe me.*

PART II
SURVIVAL

SWEDEN

Baltic Sea

ESTONIA

LATVIA

LITHUANIA

DANZIG

EAST
PRUSSIA

BELARUS

GREATER
GERMANY

Treblinka
⊗

Chelmno
⊗

Sobibor
⊗

Majdanek
⊗

Belzec ⊗

PROTECTORATE OF
BOHEMIA
AND
MORAVIA

Auschwitz
⊗

UKRAINE

POLAND

SLOVAKIA

AUSTRIA

HUNGARY

ROMANIA

CROATIA

SERBIA

Adriatic Sea

OCCUPIED POLAND, 1942

⊗   Extermination Camps

– –   Poland Boundary before
German-Soviet Pact, 1939

⊘   Germany and Occupied Territories

⊘   German Allies/Dependent States

├———┤ 150 kilometers
├———┤ 100 miles

13

GERMANY WAS WINNING THE WAR.

Adolf Hitler's military conquests reached a high point in the summer of 1942. Nazi Germany ruled a vast empire stretching from the coast of France in the west to the outskirts of the Soviet capital of Moscow in the east. German U-boats were sinking Allied supply ships in the Atlantic faster than they could be replaced.

Hitler's next major objective was the industrial city of Stalingrad, in southwest Russia. From there, the plan was for German forces to drive into the rich oil fields of the Caucasus, bringing these valuable resources under Nazi control. The German army would then continue east, linking up with the Japanese military. Japanese forces had conquered parts of eastern China, as well as most of Southeast Asia and huge stretches of the South Pacific. Together, Hitler and his Axis allies would secure complete control of Europe, North Africa, and Asia.

Then, once and for all, they could finish off Great Britain and the United States.

With victory in sight, the Nazis continued building concentrations camps all over occupied Europe. Some were slave labor camps; others were used to detain anyone perceived as an enemy to Hitler. The Nazis also shipped millions of women, men, and children from Eastern Europe to Germany, forcing them to work in German homes and factories.

These were not merely wartime measures; this was Hitler's vision for the future. This was how the world would look after the Nazi victory.

Eastern Europe and the Soviet Union would become, in Hitler's words, a "Garden of Eden" for Germany. The land would be opened to German settlers, and the Slavic people of Eastern Europe and Russia—people Hitler declared inferior to Germans—were to be nothing more than a source of labor.

And there would be no Jews. In 1942, the Nazis took their "Final Solution" to a horrific extreme, establishing new camps in occupied Poland: Belzec, Treblinka, and Sobibor. Compared to Auschwitz, these camps were small—fenced-in clearings in remote forests along railroad tracks. These places had one purpose: rapid mass murder.

Prisoners arrived on trains and were told they were stopping briefly so that their clothes and bodies could be cleaned and disinfected. Surrounded by armed guards, prisoners were separated by gender, given towels, and led into what appeared to be shower rooms. The SS guards shut the doors and pumped in carbon monoxide, using diesel engines to produce the poison gas. Dead bodies were dragged out and dumped into pits in the woods.

Stories of Nazi brutality continued to reach free countries in Europe and beyond. Newspapers reported on the mass deportations of Jews from German-occupied countries. Resistance fighters in Poland watched the trains and described their route to isolated concentration camps.

On July 2, 1942, the *New York Times* printed an article reporting that the Nazis were likely murdering Jews by the hundreds of thousands in Poland. This might seem like major news—but the piece was buried on page six of the paper. The journalist even cast doubt on his own story, citing a Jewish leader in London who thought the report, in the journalist's words, "seemed too terrible and the atrocities too inhuman to be true."

This was essentially the U.S. government's reaction as well. The State Department called the story "fantastic," treating it as a mix of exaggeration and unfounded rumor.

Of course, Americans knew there was nothing far-fetched about innocent people being locked in prison camps—it was happening at home. Two months after Japan's attack on Pearl Harbor, President Franklin Roosevelt's Executive Order 9066 authorized the removal of "any or all persons" from so-called military areas of the United States. The government forced 122,000 Japanese Americans—most of them U.S. citizens, and against whom there was no evidence of disloyalty—out of their homes on the West Coast and into internment camps surrounded by barbed wire and guard towers.

This is not to equate American internment camps with Nazi killing centers. Both were rooted in prejudice and lies, but they were very different sorts of crimes.

In late July, American Jewish leaders held a massive rally in New York's Madison Square Garden to sound the alarm that the Jews of Europe were in immediate danger of annihilation. President

Roosevelt sent a message of sympathy, vowing the American people would "hold the perpetrators of these crimes to strict accountability in a day of reckoning which will surely come."

But for the time being, these were merely words. Roosevelt's position was that America's sole focus would be on defeating Germany and its allies on the battlefield. Anything else was a dangerous distraction.

Might it have made a difference if there had been a firsthand account of mass murder at camps such as Auschwitz? Maybe—but we can't say for sure. Because the world was not confronted with an eyewitness account of what the Nazis were doing at Auschwitz.

Not until Rudi Vrba brought one out himself.

"In a week's time there will be a very big event," Rudi's block senior announced one evening that summer. "We are to be visited by Reichsführer Himmler."

The block senior, a high-ranking kapo with the green triangle of a career criminal, lectured the prisoners about how to behave in front of their esteemed guest. If Himmler asked anyone about conditions in camp, they were to say, "I am very happy here, thank you, Sir." Nothing more.

Everyone was tense all week. Even the SS men were fidgety. When the big day came, a sunny day in mid-July, the prisoners lined up outside. Rudi was placed in the front row of his group. Probably, he figured, because he was seventeen and still relatively healthy.

Kommandant Rudolf Höss and the camp's other top officers stood by the front gate in freshly pressed uniforms and gleaming black boots. The camp orchestra sat on a raised platform, holding their instruments. An SS man watching the road signaled to the conductor, who lifted his baton. The musicians began the "Triumphal March" from Verdi's opera *Aida* as a black limousine rolled through the gates.

Himmler stepped out of the back seat. He stood for a moment, enjoying the music.

So this was Heinrich Himmler, Rudi thought. This was the head of the SS, the mass murderer who controlled the lives of everyone in camp. A monster? Yes, but ordinary looking, with round glasses and an ill-fitting black uniform.

Höss greeted his honored guest with clicked heels and the Nazi salute. The men talked briefly, sharing a laugh, then began inspecting the prisoners. Himmler strolled toward Rudi's group with a phony smile pasted on his face. Was he bored already? Feigning interest to be polite?

Himmler came so close that Rudi could have reached out and touched him. Their eyes even met for a second, "cold, impersonal eyes," Rudi thought. He got the sense the man had not actually seen him.

Rudolf Höss then led his boss on a tour of the rapidly expanding Auschwitz complex. Himmler looked over models for large brick buildings planned for a new section of camp, Birkenau, about two miles from the Auschwitz main camp.

They drove to the camp's railroad ramp as a train arrived with Jewish prisoners from Holland. Himmler watched SS doctors perform a so-called selection, quickly looking over each new arrival. Young, fit-looking men and women were chosen for forced labor. Everyone else, about 450 men, women, and children, were loaded onto trucks and driven to a whitewashed farmhouse set among fruit trees on the Birkenau side of the camp property. A sign on the farm-house door read DISINFECTION ROOM. In fact, this was one of two houses that Höss had converted to gas chambers, giving him added capacity beyond the crematorium.

"Himmler very carefully observed the entire process of annihi-lation," Höss would later say of the visit. He'd recall that his boss "made no comment about the extermination process. He just looked on in total silence."

That evening, Himmler joined camp officers for wine and cigars. The SS chief was pleased with what he had seen. At the end of the two-day inspection, he promoted Höss and urged him to push for-ward quickly with the new buildings in Birkenau.

He reminded Höss that every means must be used to prevent prisoners from escaping.

14

THE TRAINS KEPT COMING THROUGH the summer of 1942. The population of prisoners at Auschwitz rose to over twenty thousand. The majority were Jews, with smaller groups of Polish anti-Nazis, Soviet prisoners of war, and Roma people—another group Hitler had absurdly declared "racially inferior."

Most of the prisoners were men, though sometimes, while marching to work, Rudi saw groups of young female prisoners. They too were being marched to some sort of forced labor. They too had shaved heads and hungry faces.

Rudi had seen enough of Auschwitz to know he was lucky to be working in the food warehouse and lucky to be working for Franz. Unlike so many of the kapos, Franz was never cruel or senselessly violent. He was even capable of stunning acts of kindness. At the warehouse, when there were no SS guards lurking, he'd kick over a jar of jam or pickled vegetables.

"How careless of me!" he'd say, turning his back, as Rudi and the others raced to eat the food off the floor.

This was literally lifesaving. No one could live more than a few months on the bread and broth given to prisoners, especially while doing long days of hard labor. Every morning Rudi saw bodies piled onto carts and pulled to the crematorium building.

As they marched to and from work, Rudi and Josef Erdelyi watched for any weakness in the camp's defenses, any flaw that might give them even the tiniest chance to slip away. Ipi Müller, as always, spoke incessantly of his talented son. Ipi remained convinced that Filip was a musician in the camp orchestra and found great comfort in this. His boy, at least, was being spared the very worst of Auschwitz.

In fact, Filip *was* in Auschwitz. But he was not in the orchestra.

Filip Müller, a slim, dark-haired man of twenty, had arrived at Auschwitz about two months before his father and Rudi. He'd been put to work on street construction. That changed suddenly one terrible Sunday.

The prisoners were not marched to work on Sundays, though the day brought its own special miseries. The kapos in Filip's block were a gang of professional criminals who entertained themselves by commanding Jewish prisoners to perform pointless "exercises." Standing in columns, Filip and the other prisoners were ordered to put on and remove their caps over and over and over again. Anyone who couldn't keep up was plagued with added drills:

"Lie down!"

"Get up!"

"Crawl!"

"Get up!"

"Jump!"

Kapos stalked their prey, swinging clubs. As usual, SS guards looked on with only mild interest.

Filip willed his way through a morning of this madness. He lined up with the other prisoners in front of the vats of morning tea. The prisoners were drained and winded, desperate for a drink. The kapos made sure everyone was watching. Then they tipped the barrels of tea into the gutter.

Next came delousing. Prisoners stood in the yard searching their clothes for lice, which spread typhus, one of the biggest killers in camp. The men then washed without soap and had the stubble torn from their cheeks and head by dull razors.

Lunch was rotting vegetables in watery broth. Filip drank his portion, feeling a bit of energy returning to his body with each swallow.

Then it was time for rest in the barracks. Prisoners crowded into their bunks and were ordered to shut up. Filip lay awake, listening to moans of pain and hunger, and snores. He envied those who were able to sleep. Tormented by thirst, he could think of nothing but getting something to drink.

The man sharing his bunk, a French Jew named Maurice, gestured out to the yard. Filip understood. The barrels of evening tea were probably already out there. Possibly unguarded. Maurice was suggesting they sneak out there right now.

This would be far too dangerous, Filip knew.

But what if the kapos decided, just for fun, to pour the evening tea onto the ground? That image was enough. Filip climbed out of his bunk.

The two men tiptoed down the stairs. They peered out the

barracks door. No kapos or SS in sight. The vats of tea were there, against the wall. Filled to the top.

Filip charged to a barrel and thrust his face into the warm liquid, drinking in enormous gulps. When he came up for air, he saw Maurice with his face in the next barrel.

Filip bent down for another drink—and felt a strong hand grip the back of his neck. He struggled to get free, but the grip tightened, holding him under. Drowning, panicking, he instinctively opened his mouth to take in air and sucked tea into his lungs. Filip felt an explosion of pain in his head, and lost consciousness.

"Get up!"

The shouting sounded miles away.

"Get cracking!"

Filip opened his eyes. He was lying on the ground, a terrible pounding in his ears. Through unfocused eyes he saw two familiar kapos standing over him, roaring at him to stand.

Filip forced himself up. He stood on shaky legs. Maurice, groaning with pain, did the same.

Guards marched Filip and Maurice down a road, through a wooden gate, and into a paved courtyard enclosed by a tall concrete wall. On one side of the yard was a low building with a red brick chimney rising above the building's flat roof.

This was the Auschwitz crematorium. Inside was the camp's gas chamber—though Filip had no way of knowing this yet.

A very young SS guard, Hans Stark, stepped out of the door, holding a horse whip.

"Get in, you swine!"

Stark flogged the prisoners down a hallway thick with the stench of burning flesh. He opened a door and shoved them into a large open space. Filip froze. There were bodies all over the floor. Women and men lying dead. Fully dressed. No visible injuries. Suitcases beside them.

"Get a move on!" Stark ordered. "Strip the stiffs!"

Only the sting of Stark's whip got Filip moving. What was he supposed to do? Undress these bodies? Most wore suits and dresses. A few wore Soviet military uniforms. Who were these people? How had so many people died so suddenly?

Disoriented with terror, only half hearing Stark's curses, Filip took in details in random order:

A fan spinning in an opening in the ceiling.

In an open suitcase, several boxes of matches from a store in Slovakia.

The body of a woman he'd gone to school with. Her name was Jolana.

Stark was screaming again: "Get out, to the corpse ovens!"

And Filip was driven into another room. Through scorching, smoky air, he could make out figures moving around, hurrying back and forth. Prisoners, he saw as his eyes adjusted, with yellow stars on their shirts. The room glowed with the flickering light of fire, and he saw bursts of flames through the open doors of huge iron incinerators. The prisoners pushed a cart up to one of the oven doors. The cart was piled with naked corpses.

"Grab this pole quickly," a prisoner told him. "Otherwise the SS man will beat you to death."

Filip lifted a steel pole with forklike points on one end. He felt searing heat on his hands and face as he reached into the oven to stoke the fire. Around him, the crew worked quickly, loading bodies onto the wheeled carts and pushing them to the oven doors. Horrified, fighting through the fog of shock, Filip needed to make a very quick decision.

He could do this work, or he could die right now. There were no other options.

"Pretending all the time to be working hard, I was trying desperately to gather new strength," Filip would later say. "My every thought, every fiber of my being, was concentrated on only one thing: to stay alive, one minute, one hour, one day, one week."

15

FROM THAT MOMENT ON FILIP was a member of what camp authorities called the Sonderkommando, or special command—the unit of prisoners forced to work in Nazi gas chambers and crematoria. Within the tall walls of the crematorium courtyard, Filip watched the Nazis develop an efficient system of mass murder.

Trains came in mainly at night. Groups of hundreds stumbled into the crematorium courtyard: middle-aged men and women, young women with children, older people panting with the effort of keeping up. Weakened and disoriented from days in ghastly boxcars, people were desperate above all for a drink of water.

"You have come here to work in the same way as our soldiers who are fighting at the front," an SS officer would announce. "Whoever can work will be treated well."

These lies were effective. The new arrivals were frightened, but hopeful. People believed they would get through this ordeal, get something to drink, and be put to work. They had learned to expect inhuman cruelty from the Nazis—still, the idea of murder by poison gas, the mass murder of children, was beyond imagination.

Officers ordered everyone to undress for a shower. Other SS men typically spoke to individuals in the crowd, asking about the type of work they did. If a man said he was a tailor, an SS man would say, "Wonderful, we need people like you. When you've had your shower, report to me at once."

Once everyone was inside, guards shut the door and slid an iron bolt into place. Guards in gas masks opened the hatches on the roof and poured in poison. The bodies were then cremated in the building's incinerators.

"And what ought we prisoners to do in this situation?"

Filip tormented himself with this question. Each time a new group arrived at the crematorium, he wondered, *What should I do? What is the right thing to do?*

He imagined himself stepping forward and shouting: "You are taking your last walk—a terrible death in the gas chamber awaits you!"

But who would believe such a claim? How would the children react?

Only one thing was certain: the SS would kill him right away. He was watching a monstrous crime and was powerless to stop it. The thought in Filip's head was that he must survive somehow. Survive and bear witness to the world.

Filip sometimes stole glances at the SS men. How was it possible for people to carry out such duties? He particularly wondered about Hans Stark, who was his own age, barely twenty. What had happened to Stark? Where did such intense hatred come from?

After the war ended, war crimes prosecutors would ask concentration camp staff these very questions.

"We were relieved of thinking, for others were doing it for us," Hans Stark would say. "After all, every third phrase was 'The Jews are to blame for everything, the Jews are our misfortune.' This was drummed into us."

Other Nazis, up to the top leaders, said essentially the same thing. Hitler's relentless lies—and the centuries of lies and conspiracy theories that had come before—created a distorted reality in which Jews were seen as less than fully human. Once the Nazis accepted that a group of people was inferior, that their lives were worthless, it seemed natural that they should be robbed and enslaved, even eliminated.

"Of course it was an unusual and monstrous order," Rudolf Höss would say of Himmler's instructions to commit mass murder at Auschwitz. "But the reasoning behind the extermination process seemed to me right. I thought no more of it at the time."

In the history of the world, this type of depraved "reasoning" is not unique to Nazi Germany.

And can we honestly say that it existed only in the past?

16

RUDI'S LIFE AT AUSCHWITZ CHANGED just as quickly as Filip's.

The trouble started one morning when a group of female prisoners marched past the food warehouse. They were very young, clearly starving. Guards fenced them into a yard behind the warehouse. Franz, the kind-hearted kapo, looked on with sympathy. He grabbed a case of Italian marmalade and walked out the door.

Stunned, Rudi ran upstairs for a better view. He watched from a window as Franz stepped up to the fence and tossed the box over the barbed wire. The glass jars broke open on the ground.

The women hesitated—then fell to their knees to scoop up the jam. It was gone in seconds.

Later that day an SS inspector counted the cases of marmalade. There were supposed to be one thousand. He counted 999. The inspector pulled prisoners aside one by one, demanding information. Rudi, Josef, and Ipi denied any knowledge of the theft, but someone talked. Franz was dragged off to the punishment block, and then the

SS man turned on the prisoners, calling them thieves and saboteurs, "vermin, trafficking in the food of men who are fighting to save civilization."

Civilization! Was that some sick attempt at humor? Rudi watched the man's face. He was dead serious.

"Tomorrow," he growled, "you will be assigned to new work."

"You're being transferred to Block Eighteen," a kapo told Rudi that evening in the barracks. "To the Buna Command."

This went for Josef Erdelyi and Ipi Müller as well. The friends didn't know what Buna was, though they'd heard it spoken of. Always with dread.

A German kapo woke the three friends at three in the morning. He hurried them through the dark camp to Block 18. The men of Buna Command were already lined up outside their barracks.

"Has everybody got bread?" another kapo asked.

Most did have small pieces, apparently saved from the night before. Rudi and his friends had none but said nothing. They knew never to call attention to themselves.

The kapo stepped up to them. "This is your first day with Buna, isn't it?"

"Yes, Herr kapo," Rudi said.

"I'll bet you have no bread."

"No, Herr kapo."

The man cursed, pulled a hunk of break from his pocket, and gave them each a piece. Rudi was grateful for the food, but took it as a bad sign.

Why is this criminal taking pity on us? What could possibly lie ahead?

"March!"

The usual force of SS guards, with their guns and dogs, watched the prisoners parade in orderly groups of one hundred through the camp's front gate. The men marched down the dark road to a railway track, where a long train of boxcars sat waiting.

The kapos clubbed the men into the cars. Rudi's entire group crammed into one car, packed so tight no one could move. The doors slammed shut. The train rocked and began moving. A man in the corner, his arm broken by a kapo's club, vomited from the pain. Someone near Rudi, suffering from severe dysentery, had no choice but to relieve himself where he stood. Something fundamental had changed, Rudi sensed. There were layers of torture at Auschwitz, and he'd just descended to a lower level.

The train stopped. The doors opened. Kapos swung their canes, pulling people from the wagon, shrieking:

"Faster, you bastards!"

"We're late!"

"Faster!"

The prisoners marched double-time down a tree-lined road. The sun was up. The morning was already hot. A man in the group in front of Rudi made a run for the trees. The SS opened fire and the man fell dead. The pace of the march never slowed.

Rudi saw the work site up ahead: an enormous clearing with building foundations, construction cranes, spinning cement machines, piles of lumber, SS men kicking kapos and kapo whips cracking, hundreds of prisoners running from place to place, always running.

Rudi's group was led to a mountain of sacks of cement mix.

"Shift these to the site over there," a kapo ordered. "Get moving! At the double! Run, you pigs, run!"

That was the entirety of the instructions.

A prisoner set a heavy bag on Rudi's shoulder. Rudi joined the column of men racing across the clearing to a spot where another crew worked at cement mixers. He dropped the bag and ran back for another, already gasping for air, coughing on cement dust.

A few more trips and Rudi's back was throbbing, his legs burning, sandy sweat streaming into his eyes. But his only focus was on moving, staying in line, avoiding notice. A man ahead of him fell. A kapo killed him with a blow to the head.

Rudi tripped on the body but kept running. He dumped his bag and went back for another.

The summer day turned scorching. Water gushed from hoses all over the site, pooling in the dirt, but no one was allowed to stop and drink. Rudi's throat and mouth were layered with dust. His vision softened. He lost track of time, of how many trips he'd made.

A whistle blew. The machines stopped. Many men fell to the ground.

A few dove for puddles in the dirt. Rudi tottered to a water tap and was about to drink when an older prisoner yanked him back.

"Don't touch that, friend," the man warned. "One mouthful and you'll get dysentery."

The man had just saved his life.

Rudi collapsed beside Josef and Ipi. Prisoners carried over barrels of tea and soup and Rudi gulped down his tiny portion. He and his friends sat together in the sun, heads between their knees, unable to muster the energy to talk.

The whistle blew.

"Back to work, you bastards!"

"Get moving!"

"On your feet! Run, run, run!"

Nothing Rudi had ever done required as much willpower as it took now to simply stand up.

Rudi was at Auschwitz as a slave laborer, a man with no rights; he'd understood that before his first morning at the construction site. Now he realized that the situation was actually much worse. The Nazis wanted his labor, yes, but they didn't care if he lived or died.

No, it was even worse. They *wanted* him to die. They wanted to work him to death. To use him up and throw him aside. He'd be replaced the moment he broke.

Rudi ran back and forth with the heavy bags, back and forth, back and forth. About an hour into the afternoon he dropped a bag by the mixing machines. It burst open, spewing powder. A man in overalls, some sort of civilian supervisor, cursed Rudi in French.

This was one of those seemingly small moments that meant the difference between life and death at Auschwitz.

Josef stepped forward and spoke to the civilian in French. This seemed to distract the man from his fury. Rudi couldn't follow the conversation, but Josef was smiling as he turned around.

"We've got a new job," he told Rudi.

Rudi and Josef worked for the French foreman for the next few hours, twisting steel wires into frames to reinforce concrete in the buildings under construction. This was easier than hauling the bags.

Rudi was not sure he'd have lived through the day without Josef's quick thinking.

When his group staggered back to the train that evening, ninety of the hundred men from that morning were still alive. They piled ten bodies into their boxcar for the ride back to Auschwitz.

It was getting dark as they marched through the main gate. Everyone was counted, living and dead. Rudi got his portion of bread with margarine and forced himself to save half for the morning. He slept with the precious hunk clutched in his fist.

17

BY THE SUMMER OF 1942, Adolf Hitler was demanding more from his Hungarian allies. Hitler expected Hungary to round up and deport its Jewish population, and this had not happened yet. An even more pressing matter was Germany's invasion of the Soviet Union. German forces had not won the quick victory Hitler had predicted, and he insisted the Hungarian army join the battle. Hungary's leaders sent two hundred thousand young men to fight under German command on the eastern front.

From her family's flat in Budapest, Gerta watched with dread as Hungarians went on with life as normal, enjoying restaurants and shows, throwing parties—Jews too, including her own Hungarian relatives. Gerta's generous aunts took her to dress shops and fancy cafés. She'd sit with them, leaving her cake untouched. Her behavior appeared ungrateful and rude. She knew that.

But what was she supposed to do? Just pretend that everything was going to be fine?

Gerta became so depressed that she was barely able to eat. She shed weight, and her periods stopped.

One of Gerta's aunts, Manci, tried to lift her niece's spirits with a season pass to a posh swimming club on Margaret Island in the Danube River, right in the middle of the city. The place had glittering pools, green lawns, and food vendors. Manci and her friends went nearly every day, and Gerta tagged along. The adults lived it up.

"I, meanwhile, sat in the sun," Gerta recalled, "watching the people around me enjoying themselves, swimming, playing table tennis, and couldn't help thinking of my friends. Were they still alive, and if so how much did they suffer?"

Rudi lined up each morning in the dark. Kapos stalked the lines, inspecting the prisoners, pointing to men who looked too sick or starved to live through the day.

"Hospital!" they'd shout.

This was just another form of death sentence. People did not come back from the "hospital." Condemned prisoners pleaded their case, insisting they were strong enough to keep going. Even if a kapo sympathized, he faced a difficult call—knowing he'd be thrashed by the SS for bringing a dying man to work.

Rudi and Josef continued twisting steel cables for the French foreman. The others were less lucky. Each evening Rudi's group carried back its dead. Some days five, some days fifteen. Each morning the group had one hundred men again.

As the familiar faces disappeared, Rudi felt a layer of numbness spreading over him. It was a protective coat, a necessary step for survival—but it could be pierced, sparking sudden bursts of pain.

This happened when Rudi looked at Ipi Müller one day and saw that his friend was fading.

There was life in Ipi's eyes. He was fighting, but his body was failing. And he was still talking about his son Filip. Still hoping to see him playing his violin in the orchestra.

Filip Müller still did not know his father was so close.

When they were not at the crematorium building, Filip and other Sonderkommando workers were locked in small cells, isolated from other prisoners. They didn't starve, at least, since it was often possible to steal—to "organize," in camp slang—scraps of food from the suitcases of new arrivals.

The SS guards looked the other way at such things. They were busy stealing more valuable items from the gas chamber victims, and besides, having workers in decent shape saved them the trouble of constantly training new crews. The crematorium crews could always be eliminated later, long before they could tell anyone in the outside world what they had seen.

Filip heard about his father when a group of prisoners was brought into the crematorium to repair its crumbling brick chimney. One of the repairmen, an older man from Slovakia, knew Filip's family, and told Filip that Ipi was in camp. Using money and jewels he organized in the crematorium, Filip bribed the kapo in charge of the repair crew to add Ipi to the team.

Father and son met in the morning in a little kapos' hut.

Ipi raised a frail hand to stroke his son's cheek. "I was looking for you all over the place," he said, "and felt sure I would find you among the musicians of the camp orchestra."

Filip felt his throat tighten. His eyes filled with tears. This good man really believed, or was making himself believe, that his son was a musician. Filip imagined himself shouting, "You are mistaken, Father! Your son Filip, the promising grammar-school boy, the budding violinist, is not a musician but one who cremates corpses. Do you hear me, Father!"

But Filip could not speak. He ran out of the hut and back to the crematorium.

Filip and Ipi met a few more times in the following weeks. Filip could see that his father was suffering from typhus. Taking an enormous risk, Filip bribed his way out of his cell on a Sunday and slipped into his father's barracks.

Rudi watched from a distance. Ipi was near the end, that was obvious. But the man smiled as he talked with his son. He smiled even as they said goodbye.

Filip walked to Rudi. They shook hands.

"My father has told me how you've helped him," Filip said. "I want to thank you. And I want you to do me another favor."

"Of course."

"He asked me if I was in the orchestra. I told him I was."

Filip attempted a grin. Rudi saw deep misery in the expression.

"Do you know where I work?" Filip said. "In the crematorium."

He gave Rudi a quick summary of what happened in the building with the brick chimney. A detailed description of the entire process would have to wait until they had more time to talk. Rudi promised to keep Filip's secret.

A few days later, when Filip was at the crematorium, his father's body arrived on the evening truck. The men placed Ipi's body on the wheeled cart in front of the ovens. One of them began reciting the Mourner's Kaddish, a prayer said in honor and memory of the dead.

18

RUDI AND JOSEF CONTINUED TWISTING wire frames at the Buna construction site—"buna" was synthetic rubber, which would be produced at this factory when it was completed. By their fifth week at the site, the two friends were the only ones left from the group of one hundred they'd started with.

They weren't sure how long they could hold on. Without enough calories to fuel their bodies, their organs were weakening, their muscles shrinking. They were just seventeen but could feel themselves beginning to break down.

The next crisis came quickly.

It was a Wednesday, an important day for Rudi and Josef because on Wednesdays when they got back to camp, the Buna prisoners were given a piece of salami. They got back after dark, as usual. But unlike normal nights, prisoners from other barracks were standing outside as if for roll call. Rudi's group took its place. They stood for hours. No explanation. No food. Rudi fell asleep standing.

He woke to a demonic scene: SS guards shining flashlights on prisoners' legs and barking: "Run! Run! Run!"

The men stagger-ran maybe twenty yards, turned, and raced back.

A high-ranking officer looked on, sending prisoners to one side or the other with a jerk of his thumb.

"Run!"

Rudi burst forward on unsteady legs.

Josef ran next, stumbling and nearly falling.

Confused and gasping, both were sent to one side, where about forty other men were huddled. Rudi looked around. These men were feverish and shivering from typhus, barely able to stand.

This was a test. Rudi and Josef had just failed. They weren't sick, just famished and exhausted, but there'd be no chance to explain.

They'd just been sentenced to death.

Other prisoners, those who "passed," were lined up nearby. But with so many kapos and SS men around, there was no way Rudi and Josef could sneak over to the safe group. Now there were about eighty men in their group. When they got to one hundred, they'd be marched away.

"You bloody bastards! What the hell are you doing here!"

A kapo, a man Rudi and Josef knew. You couldn't call him a friend in this context, but for whatever reason, he decided to keep them alive.

Smacking the teenagers on the back with his club, he roared at them, "Don't you know you're supposed to be with that bunch over there?" He shoved them into a group of "healthy" prisoners. "You're lucky, boys," he whispered. "Look."

The group Rudi had been in a few seconds before was marching to the crematorium. The building he'd heard about from Filip Müller.

The selection continued all night and into the morning. Amid the chaos, Rudi heard someone speaking Slovak, an older prisoner who seemed to know a bit more about what was going on. Rudi introduced himself.

The man was Laco Fischer, a dentist, in camp for five months. A real achievement in a place where most lived half that long.

"You want to know what's happening?" Laco asked Rudi. "Half the camp has been murdered and the work commands are being reorganized." This was actually an opportunity, Laco explained. Certain desirable jobs would be coming open. "I hear," he said, "they're looking for men in Canada Command."

Rudi and Josef looked at each other. They'd heard Canada Command spoken of almost as a mythical land. Though never with details, or any explanation of the nickname.

"What's it like?" Rudi asked.

There was food, Laco told him. Butter and chocolate, sausages and sardines, even bananas! Laco had worked there a short time. He was going to try to get back and offered to put in a word for Rudi and Josef.

"But remember," he added, "in Canada you live on the edge of a precipice."

"What do you do there? What's the work like?"

"It's tough. Let's leave it at that."

Rudi was in. Josef too. Food was life here, at least a chance at life.

Laco introduced them to a kapo. The man looked them over, then pointed to the barbed wire fence. "Run for that wire."

Rudi and Josef ran, praying the SS wouldn't think they were try-ing to escape.

They ran more steadily this time and were accepted. Another kapo, a German criminal named Bruno, took charge of the group. Bruno marched them to a washroom for a shower, and then to a new barracks. Each prisoner got a blanket and, incredibly, his own bunk. Rudi almost felt lucky—but wished someone would answer his ques-tions about Canada.

"You'll see," they told him.

Or: "Why worry? You won't survive very long!"

Layers beneath layers. There were so many levels of horror in this place. So much, Rudi realized, that he still did not know.

19

"CLEARING COMMAND—FORWARD!"

So that was Canada's official name: Clearing Command. Bruno led Rudi's group past the SS and their dogs, and out beneath the camp's main archway.

"Stick close to me," Laco Fischer, the friendly dentist, whispered in Rudi's ear. "Do what I do. And don't eat too much."

Eat too much! Was Laco joking?

Bruno marched his men into a large courtyard enclosed in barbed wire. Around the yard were several warehouse buildings, and guards in watchtowers. Rudi's eyes darted around the huge space, taking in strange details:

Towering stacks of trunks, rucksacks, suitcases.

A pile of blankets, just blankets. Thousands of them.

Baby strollers, enough for a city.

Pots and pans piled into a mountain.

Women running around the yard, fairly healthy-looking prisoners, their arms full of clothes.

Women sitting on long benches squeezing tubes of toothpaste into metal buckets.

There was no time to figure any of this out. An SS officer named Richard Wiegleb, clearly the ruler of this bizarre kingdom, stepped onto a balcony outside one of the buildings to survey his subjects.

"To work!" he roared in German.

Two other SS men, Graf and König, charged among the workers. "To work! To work!"

Dodging their boots and canes, Rudi followed more experienced men to a pile of luggage. Each man grabbed two suitcases, ran into one of the storerooms, and dropped the bags on a blanket spread on the floor. One team of prisoners ripped the bags open as they arrived. Another sorted the stuff onto separate blankets: clothing, shoes, glasses, food, kitchen utensils, medicine, money and jewelry, toys, books, family photos.

This was people's luggage, Rudi realized. Prisoners arrived at camp with luggage, suitcases stuffed with everything they could carry.

"Faster, you bastards," the SS men roared. "Faster!"

Rudi ran back outside for another load. On about his tenth trip back and forth, a bag slipped from his arms and fell. Food spilled out. Apples. A piece of salami.

Rudi stopped and stared at the glorious sight.

Graf and König were on him in a second, beating him with their canes. As Rudi grabbed the bag and started running, he saw a prisoner snatch up the salami and shove it in his mouth. The man had never stopped running. The SS men saw nothing.

Here was a lesson worth learning. *Steal only what someone else drops*, Rudi told himself. *Snatch fast beneath the cloak of another man's beating.*

* * *

Wiegleb spent the day on his balcony, sipping beer, watching everything. The pace of the work never slowed.

Partway through Rudi's first morning in Canada Command, Laco's warning about the dangerous temptation of food was made clear. König grabbed a man out of line and ordered, "Dump your luggage. Don't move!"

König reached into the prisoner's pocket and pulled out an apple and a piece of bread.

"Stealing, are you? I'll teach you manners, you swine!"

Rudi never stopped running back and forth from the yard to the warehouse, but caught glimpses as he passed the SS goons lashing the prisoner with their canes, beating him until he fell unconscious to the floor.

The same thing happened several times that day. Bleeding prisoners were left on the ground to die. The work went on, never slowed. Rudi was disgusted, horrified—but used the beatings as opportunities to snatch mouthfuls of food.

When the long day finally ended, the prisoners lined up in orderly rows. Wiegleb came down from his balcony and walked among them, looking each man over. "You," he commanded, jabbing his cane. "And you, and you. Stand out!"

Graf and König searched the unlucky chosen.

One had two lemons. Twenty lashes, Wiegleb ordered.

One had a men's shirt stuffed under his prison shirt. Twenty-five lashes.

A tin of sardines. Twenty-five lashes.

The survivors carried the dead back to their barracks. They lined up and were searched again. Another man was found with a stolen shirt. An SS guard beat him to death.

Was it worth it? Rudi wondered. He'd been able to grab a few bites of food, but how long could that last? Everyone who'd risked taking more than a mouthful was now lying dead in the mud.

Or maybe not.

Back in the barracks after roll call, Rudi watched in utter amazement as prisoners pulled lemons from inside their clothes. Cans of sardines. Sausages. Soap. Aspirin. So it *was* possible to organize goods in Canada, Rudi saw.

The block kapos came in to take their cut of the loot. A routine day at Canada Command.

When prisoners carried what was left of the stuff outside, Rudi followed. He watched, deeply moved, as the men drifted among crowds of prisoners, slipping friends lifesaving morsels of food, handing small bottles of medicine to prisoners who'd been doctors back in the real world.

This is how people stayed alive here. This is how they helped each other live another day.

Whatever the risk of working in Canada, Rudi decided, it was definitely worth it.

After a week in Canada Command, Rudi could see a bit more of the picture. First of all, the name: it was because many people from Central and Eastern Europe had emigrated to Canada before the war and done well there, found work and freedom. The word "Canada" came to represent a far-off land of plenty.

Why take the trouble to sort the goods so carefully? Because the purpose of Auschwitz was not only forced labor and murder. It was also theft on a massive scale. Everything was packed onto trains and sent to Germany.

Even the toothpaste made sense, the women squeezing tubes into pails. Rudi saw it a few times as he ran past—someone would find a diamond hidden in the tube, or a wad of cash rolled in plastic.

The cash went into the pile of money prisoners pulled from the luggage. With hopes of starting over somewhere new, people had exchanged their life savings for widely accepted currencies: U.S. dollars, British pounds, Swiss francs. Every day the cash filled a huge suitcase, often packed so full one SS man had to stand on it while another latched it shut.

Which is not to say everything made it into the suitcase. The SS men stole openly in view of the prisoners. Wiegleb took tin cans full of jewels up to his office, and there was no knowing how many never made it onto the train.

Rudi once found a roll of U.S. hundreds inside a hunk of bread. In a small and wildly dangerous act of defiance, he sneaked the money into the latrine and tossed it into the pool of filth.

After the clothes were sorted, and yellow stars removed, they too were packed up for shipment to Germany. Everything went to the Nazis, except for the category of goods deemed "worthless"—books, letters, and photographs, which went into a separate pile to be burned.

A few weeks after his transfer to Canada Command, the kapo Bruno gave Rudi what counted as a promotion, moving him inside and putting him to work carrying blankets full of clothing from the storeroom where they were unpacked to another room where women did a more careful search and sorting.

It was a mixed blessing. Rudi was able to sneak food to the women, and they shared what they found with him in exchange. But in Auschwitz every benefit came with a new danger. The kapos began using Rudi as a courier, slipping him gifts for particular women. Rudi knew he'd be beaten to death if caught with the gifts, but it was not possible to refuse a kapo's demand.

It got worse. Bruno fell for a young kapo named Hermione, an Austrian blonde who patrolled the clothes-sorting workshop in tall black boots with a whip in her hand. Pretty soon Rudi was bringing her presents from Bruno, an orange on one trip, a bottle of perfume, a bar of fancy soap.

Day after day, Wiegleb watched from his balcony.

Rudi knew it was only a matter of time until he was caught.

20

IT HAPPENED PRETTY MUCH HOW he expected.

Rudi was carrying a load of clothes, on the run as always, when Wiegleb called for him to stop. Rudi stood still, watching the SS officer slowly descend the steps to the warehouse floor.

"Dump it!"

Rudi let his blanket fall. Wiegleb did a quick search.

Clothes. Only clothes.

Rudi made maybe three hundred trips a day back and forth, carrying contraband on only a select few.

Wiegleb hit Rudi anyway, but not too hard. "Carry on," he ordered. "And make it snappy."

Rudi gathered his bundle and ran. He figured he'd be left alone for a while. But on the next trip the voice called down from the balcony again. Again, Wiegleb took his sweet time coming down the stairs.

"Dump it!"

Another inspection. Nothing but clothes. The same thing happened on the next trip. Rudi had never seen Wiegleb do this.

Bruno watched from a safe distance.

When Rudi went back for his next load, Bruno approached. "He won't stop you for the rest of the day now," Bruno whispered. "Take some stuff over to Hermione."

Some stuff? It looked like Bruno had robbed a department store. He'd laid out French perfume and soap, German frankfurters, sardines from Portugal, chocolate from Switzerland.

Rudi had no choice. Bruno could murder him just as quickly as the SS. He loaded everything into his bundle of clothes and dashed across the warehouse.

"You—halt!"

Rudi kept running. It was his only hope.

"You, you bastard!" Wiegleb screamed. "Drop that blanket before you're shot!"

Rudi stopped. He turned to face Wiegleb. He could see it on the Nazi's face—he knew. He was enjoying this. He'd been setting Rudi up.

The blanket fell to the floor and opened.

Rudi woke up in his bunk the next morning. At first, he had no idea how he got there.

"You did all right yesterday."

Bruno, the kapo, was standing over him with an odd look on his face. Fear? Respect?

Slowly, the scene from the day before re-formed in Rudi's mind.

The blanket fell to the floor and opened.

Wiegleb studied the loot with the world's phoniest expression of shock. "What a strange collection of clothes!" he practically sang. "I wonder what lucky girl was going to get this little haul."

Rudi made up his mind to say nothing.

Wiegleb called Bruno over. Bruno appeared genuinely shocked. "You stinking, thieving pig!" he roared, smacking Rudi with his stick.

"Leave this to me," Wiegleb snapped, putting the kapo in his place. "He's going to tell me where he got this loot, even if they're his last words."

Josef and the other prisoners ran back and forth with their loads, always running, glancing as they passed, powerless to help. Rudi saw Hermione across the storeroom, watching from a distance. Her life was on the line as well.

The SS thugs Graf and König marched up to do their part. Rudi knew what was coming. He'd seen it so many times. He was ordered to bend over.

Wiegleb's cane landed like lightning, with an explosion of pain. Rudi fell forward, but König kicked him back into position.

"Who gave it to you?"

Another vicious blow.

"Who gave it to you?"

Once Wiegleb started, he didn't stop. Rudi knew this. But he refused to speak. It wouldn't help; Bruno could finish him off later just as easily. And anyway, he wasn't going to give in. He just wasn't.

Wiegleb lowered his voice to a menacing whisper. "Who . . . gave . . . it . . . to . . . you?"

Another lash of the cane. More kicks from Wiegleb's goons.

Rudi counted them at first. Five, six, seven . . . Wiegleb was in no hurry. He'd repeat his question, then hit, swinging harder as his frustration grew. Nine, ten, eleven . . . The sounds of the warehouse faded in and out, as if someone were playing with the dial of a radio. Rudi's vision bounced and blurred. Each blow landed with a brand-new shock of pain.

"Who gave it to you? Who gave it to you? Who gave it to you?"

He only sensed the words. Dancing red lights flashed through his closed eyelids. Yellow lights, purple lights.

Then nothing.

And here he was a day later. In his bunk with Bruno standing over him.

"He couldn't believe it when you wouldn't talk," Bruno said. "D'you know, I think he had a bit of admiration for you in the end."

Rudi's whole body felt broken. It was torture even to breathe. "I can't get up," he managed to say. "I can't work."

Bruno understood the seriousness of this. If you can't work, you die.

He said he'd cover for Rudi. Wiegleb would assume he was dead, and Bruno had enough pull with other kapos to keep Rudi hidden in the barracks for a few days.

Josef stepped to the bunk. He lifted Rudi's head and held a cup to his friend's lips.

Lemonade. The unbelievable taste of real lemon. Real sugar. Josef had risked his life to bring Rudi these few precious ounces.

Nearly fifteen hundred miles to the east, German forces were still trying to fight their way into the Soviet city of Stalingrad. Adolf Hitler was certain that the fall of Stalingrad would knock the Soviet

Union out of the war, giving the Nazis complete domination of Europe.

German bombers reduced Stalingrad to rubble. Axis commanders hurled waves of troops and tanks into the ruins, but Soviet defenders held fast, fighting back from basements, from the skeletal remains of buildings, inflicting heavy casualties on the invaders.

In Hungary, Gerta and her parents listened to war updates on the radio. The news made it sound as if Axis forces were closing in on a decisive victory.

But Gerta could sense things beginning to change. Hungarian soldiers continued to leave for the Soviet front. Hitler was demanding a steady stream of supplies from his allies, which caused food shortages in Hungary. The government began rationing food, but since they were in the country illegally Gerta's family was not eligible for the ration stamps needed to purchase groceries. "We had to buy ration books on the black market," she recalled, "and that was yet another danger."

Gerta was determined to help her parents. She couldn't apply for jobs without identity papers, but her mother arranged for both of them to knit gloves and scarves for a nearby shop—work they could do in the safety of their apartment. The work helped lift Gerta's mood. She was glad to be busy, and spent a bit of the money she earned on private French lessons.

Nothing would really improve, though, until Hitler was beaten on the battlefield. When might that be? No one could say.

"At this stage," Gerta would recall of the fall of 1942, "we could not imagine that we would live to see Hitler's defeat."

21

FROM INSIDE AUSCHWITZ, RUDI COULD not know who was winning the war. He'd catch an occasional glimpse of a guard's newspaper, but of course those were Nazi-approved stories and not to be trusted. One thing seemed fairly clear: there was no end in sight.

Rudi's immediate problem, as he healed from Wiegleb's beating, was that he needed to get back to work. But where?

"I can't bring you back to work with me, that's for sure," Bruno told Rudi. "If Wiegleb sees you alive, he'll kill you."

Bruno's solution was to send Rudi to the "ramp," which was also staffed by prisoners from Canada Command.

Here was another layer of Auschwitz. Another piece of the puzzle.

The ramp was a long wooden platform along the train tracks coming into camp. Situated between Auschwitz main camp and Birkenau, it was almost like a train station. But not in any normal sense. Trains rolled in slowly, usually at night. Dozens of armed SS guards surrounded the ramp. Bright lights illuminated the tracks, and Rudi could see faces in the barred windows of the boxcars. Passengers looking out, wondering where they were, why they were here.

When the train stopped, SS officers unlocked the cars and slid the doors open.

"Everybody out!"

People staggered onto the platform, blinded by the lamps' glare, weak from hunger and thirst, trying to stick with their families.

Trains came in from all over Europe; the longer they'd been traveling, the more horrific the conditions in the cars. Nazi officers sometimes faked sympathy as they looked into the wagons, shaking their heads in disgust at the overflowing buckets of waste, the dead lying on layers of luggage.

"Good God," they'd say. "This is inhuman!"

Everyone was told to line up. An SS doctor moved down the platform making a quick selection, sending strong young men and young women without children to one side—chosen, Rudi knew, because they looked fit enough to survive two or three months of forced labor.

The others, 80 to 90 percent of each transport, were never registered at Auschwitz. This included all elderly and middle-aged men and women, all children, and young women with children. Mothers, the Nazis had learned from experience, would not allow themselves to be separated from their children without a violent struggle. It was easier, the Nazis decided, to keep them together.

This entire group, several thousand on some transports, walked down a wooden staircase and into trucks parked alongside the ramp.

Then the SS men ordered Rudi's crew to get to work. Their first job was to deal with the dead left on the train. Running, as always, Rudi and another prisoner picked up bodies and carried them to a truck. After that, they unloaded the luggage. The dead went to the crematorium. The luggage went to the Canada warehouses.

Rudi was sometimes able to steal a bite of food from a bag. He'd eat while running, or slip the morsel to a friend who needed it even more.

Filip Müller had told Rudi about the gas chamber in the Auschwitz crematorium. Combining this with everything he'd experienced, Rudi was now able to see the bigger picture. Most of the Jews who arrived by trains were murdered right away. The Nazis had carefully planned every step of the process.

Deception was the key. People would do anything to stay with their families, endure any misery to give their children a chance to live. They were forced onto trains, but were together at least, and believed they were going to be resettled, put to work. They arrived at Auschwitz days later, sometimes five or even ten days later, weakened, disoriented, dying for a drink of water—Rudi knew this from his own experiences on transport trains. It was all part of the plan. The SS officers who opened the trains took advantage by acting as though they were there to help.

"Ladies and gentlemen, we are so sorry for the inconvenience which was caused by some idiot who organized this journey," they'd say. "Would you please get out and please don't get in touch with those criminals"—meaning Rudi and the other prisoners—"they are here only for taking luggage."

Or sometimes they swung canes and shouted. That seemed to depend on the schedule, on how many more trains were coming in that day. Rudi could tell from the mood of the SS officers how busy a night it was going to be.

In any case, no matter the officers' mood, by the time passengers arrived at Auschwitz it was too late to help them. Rudi and the other ramp workers were warned never to talk to passengers. Some defied the order, whispering what they hoped might be lifesaving advice:

Stand upright.

Don't admit to being under sixteen or over forty.

Leave young children with elderly relatives and stand alone.

Some teens under sixteen made it through the selection. Parents with young kids faced impossible split-second decisions.

One night on the ramp, Rudi heard a prisoner warn an older woman what was in store for those deemed unfit for work.

The woman turned to an SS officer. "One of those criminals said that we are going to die," she protested. "What does he mean? What's happening?"

"Please, madam, calm yourself," the officer told her. "Nothing is going to happen to you."

The woman spun to look for the prisoner who'd warned her. Two SS men had already dragged him behind the train and killed him.

Rudi worked on the ramp through the fall of 1942 and into the winter. He managed to avoid Richard Wiegleb, who rarely left his balcony in the warehouse.

The transports kept coming, some with a thousand people, others with five thousand. Rudi listened for talk of gas chambers among arriving prisoners, but never heard the words. He was amazed at how well the Nazis were hiding traces of their crimes.

Rudi often felt the instinct to attack SS men, especially when he saw them hitting children. He was still strong enough to hurt at least one of them before they shot him.

But would that change anything?

What would give his life meaning, Rudi decided—give his death meaning, if it came to that—would be to find some way to warn people *before* it was too late.

He counted the trains as they came in, memorizing details about how many people were on each and where they were from. These were not merely statistics to Rudi, but vivid images of specific faces. Looks of confusion and exhaustion, fear and hope. Family members separated, watching each other walk in different directions. Children standing alone, searching the crowd for their parents.

As he'd done for nearly a year, Rudi thought endlessly about escape. But his own freedom was no longer the goal. Someone needed to sound the alarm. Someone needed to get out and tell the world what was happening in Auschwitz.

Rudi decided he would be the one to do it.

He was eighteen years old.

22

BY THE END OF 1942, more than forty countries were fighting in World War II, with tens of millions of soldiers deployed worldwide. The outcome of the war was very much in doubt—though the Allies were beginning to make progress.

In the Solomon Islands of the South Pacific, U.S. Marines had landed on the Japanese-held island of Guadalcanal, sparking a vicious battle that would be a major turning point in the war in the Pacific. The Allies would go on to take the island and begin the long, bloody process of driving Japanese forces back to Japan's mainland.

In North Africa, American troops had joined the British in the fight against the Axis powers. This would lead to another victory for the Allies in the months ahead, setting up an Allied invasion of Italy.

In the Soviet Union, winter weather set in at Stalingrad. German troops were desperately short of supplies, especially warm clothing—Hitler had refused to believe it would take this long to crush the Soviet Union. He denied his generals' requests to pull back, declaring, "Where the German soldier sets foot, there he remains!"

In November, Soviet generals launched a massive counterattack across the snowy plains outside the city.

None of the news—what little Rudi saw of it—made the end of the war seem any closer. He and Josef Erdelyi were going to escape, or die trying. That was decided.

Was it possible to break out of this place? That was unknown. The challenge was to stay alive long enough to find a plan.

As winter hit Auschwitz, another wave of typhus swept through the camp's crowded barracks. Rudi hoped he was young enough, maybe still strong enough, to escape the dreaded disease. No such luck. He knew the symptoms all too well. Chills and fever. Light-headed dizziness. Wobbly imbalance when running.

He told Josef he was sick—and could see that his friend was even worse off.

At roll call the next morning, a camp clerk called the numbers of prisoners who were to report to the hospital. Rudi evaded notice that day. Josef's number was called.

"There must be a mistake," Josef said. "I'm going to work."

"Come on," the clerk said. "You've got typhus."

"I'm all right, I tell you," Josef insisted.

This was life-and-death. Everyone knew what happened to people who could no longer work.

Two kapos stepped forward with their clubs. Josef continued to protest as they dragged him out of line and shoved him into the group of sick men. He was still fighting, trying to rip free of the kapos' grasp, as they marched the group toward the hospital.

Rudi watched from his place in line. He and Josef had been inseparable since the train to Majdanek. They'd endured Buna together—Rudi may not have even made it through the first day if Josef hadn't gotten them that job with the French civilian. They'd survived months in Canada Command, always watching out for each other. They were going to escape together.

Rudi would save his friend. After work that day, he stuffed his shirt with a small fortune of stolen luxuries: lemons, chocolate, cigarettes. He hurried to the hospital and offered the registrar, a camp prisoner, a fistful of cigarettes in exchange for information about Josef.

The man checked his registration book. "Nobody of that number here."

"But he was sent down this morning," Rudi said.

"This morning? With the typhus bunch?"

Yes, that bunch, Rudi said.

The man closed his book. They'd all been "seen" by an SS doctor, he explained.

Rudi didn't abandon hope until two days later, when a prisoner who worked in the hospital filled him in on the final details. "You mean the big, blond Slovak?" the prisoner asked in response to Rudi's questions. "He fought the kapos and made a break for the wires. They shot him just as he got there."

Rudi's temperature soared. He could barely stand. There was no way he'd get through another day on the ramp. He turned to Bruno for help.

"I'm sorry for you," the kapo said, "but it's not my fault, is it?"

In other words, *I paid my debt to you. We're even. Don't ask again.*

Rudi's last hope was Laco Fischer, who'd gotten him into Canada Command. They spoke at night in the barracks. Rudi might be able to avoid notice in the Canada warehouses, Laco figured. But how was he going to get there? How was he going to march past all those SS officers who inspected the ranks each morning, yanking the weakest prisoners out of the line?

"Maybe you could prop me up?" Rudi suggested.

That made Laco laugh. In front of all those Nazi guards?

Neither spoke for a minute.

"You never know," Laco finally said. "It might work."

They tried it the next morning. Marching toward the gates in tight formation, Laco and another friend each held firmly to one of Rudi's arms. As they neared the most observant SS officers, Laco whispered, "Ready?"

"Ready."

They let go. Rudi willed his legs to move in steady steps. He made it through the gate. His friends grabbed him just before he toppled over. They got to Canada, and Laco hustled Rudi to the clothes-sorting workshop.

Hermione was there, with her black boots and whip, policing her domain. She looked at Rudi, saw the condition he was in. She remembered what he'd done, how he'd refused to give her name to Wiegleb.

In a feverish blur, Rudi felt himself being lifted by several of the women prisoners, carried up an enormous mound of clothes and set down on the top of the pile. He was right in the middle of the warehouse, but invisible from the floor.

Women checked on him every few hours. They brought him

lemonade and medicine. That evening he managed to march unnoticed back into camp.

Rudi spent the next few workdays atop the mountain of clothes. His
friends and Hermione, along with women whose names he'd never
know, risked their lives to keep him alive.

When he was strong enough to work, friends arranged the relatively easy job of sorting goods in a corner of a warehouse, out of
sight of Wiegleb's balcony. One of his jobs was to burn "useless"
paper items found in people's luggage. He was stacking the stuff one
day when he noticed something. An interesting book.

A children's atlas of the world.

Rudi had to have it. A page of it, anyway.

He glanced around. He grabbed the book, flipped to a map of
Poland, tore out the page, and shoved it in his shirt. Rudi raced to the
latrine and pulled out the paper. He couldn't keep such an incrimi-
nating piece of evidence. He'd have to study it quickly right now, in
the dim light of the stinking outhouse.

He scanned place names. And there was the town of Oświęcim
in southern Poland—the Germans called it Auschwitz.

The town sat near the meeting point of the Vistula River and one
of its tributaries, the Sola. The Sola flowed in a wavy north-south line.
Rudi followed it down to the mountainous border of Slovakia. How
far? Fifty miles, maybe a bit more. A manageable distance. He noted
the towns along the river, committing every detail to his remarkable
memory.

Then he ripped up the paper and dropped the pieces into the
latrine.

Finally, Rudi knew exactly where he was. He knew the route he'd need to travel to get home to Slovakia. He'd hardly be safe there, but he'd at least have a chance of blending in. He'd have a chance of finding people who might help him warn the world.

None of this changed the basic fact that Rudi was deep inside occupied Poland, locked in the most heavily guarded prison camp in Europe. The level of security had perplexed Rudi at first. Now, based on everything he'd learned, it made sense.

The Nazis were not really guarding prisoners at Auschwitz. They were guarding the secret of their massive crimes.

23

IN JANUARY 1943, U.S. PRESIDENT Franklin Roosevelt and British Prime Minister Winston Churchill met in Casablanca, Morocco, to chart a path toward Allied victory in World War II. Roosevelt announced to the world that there was only one acceptable outcome: the unconditional surrender of Germany, Japan, and Italy.

Flying from bases in Britain, British and U.S. bombers pounded targets inside Nazi Germany. Roosevelt and Churchill agreed that the next step would be an Allied invasion of Italy, which they saw as the weak link in the Axis alliance.

In the Soviet Union, the fight still raged at Stalingrad. The Soviet Red Army lost more than one million soldiers killed or wounded in this single campaign, but continued to attack. The Soviets surrounded a large section of the invading German army, forcing its surrender in early February. German soldiers staggered out of their trenches starving and frostbitten, rags tied around their heads for warmth.

When Hitler got news of the defeat, he stared into his bowl of soup, too rattled to throw one of his typical tantrums. This was his first serious setback, and a major turning point of World War II in Europe.

Still, unconditional surrender was a long way off. For the Allies, defeating Hitler would require a Soviet advance across Eastern Europe *and* an Allied invasion of German-occupied Western Europe. U.S. General Dwight Eisenhower was preparing plans for a massive landing on the northwestern coast of France.

But that invasion—D-Day, as it would be known—was nearly a year and a half away.

Meanwhile, Heinrich Himmler raced to complete the task Hitler had given him, even when it meant competing with the German military for scarce resources. "I need your help and support," Himmler wrote to the Nazi transportation minister. "If I am to wind things up quickly, I must have more trains for transports."

As soon as he was strong enough, Rudi returned to work on the railroad ramp—a safe distance from the SS officer who'd tried to beat him to death. Or so he thought.

He was running along the platform with a rolled-up rug on his shoulder when he spotted Richard Wiegleb, notebook in hand, watching prisoners load carpets onto a train bound for Germany. Rudi could hardly turn and run the other way. There was nothing to do but stay in line.

He jogged up to the open boxcar. Wiegleb's gaze rested on him, and Rudi could almost see the thought process. *Who is this Jewish kid? I know him from somewhere . . .*

Wiegleb got it. His mouth opened slightly. His eyes narrowed into what you could almost call a smile. "It is really you! I didn't think it was possible. And just look how fit you are, you old swine!"

Rudi braced for a violent strike.

The Nazi stared at him a moment longer, then turned and shouted, "Come on, you bastards! This is not a holiday camp! Get loading!"

Rudi dropped his carpet on the pile and ran back to the truck for another.

In the gangster logic of camp, Rudi realized, this incident might actually improve his chances of survival. An SS officer had chosen not to murder him on the spot. Lower-ranking guards, as well as kapos, would take notice.

In another bizarre twist, Wiegleb saved Rudi's entire command from immediate death.

Rudi never learned the exact details, but there was some dispute between Wiegleb and higher-ups in the SS, who couldn't help but notice how much stealing was going on in Canada Command. Naturally, the prisoners were blamed. Camp authorities wanted to gas the entire group and start over. Wiegleb objected. Not because he wanted to save his prisoners, but because he didn't feel like training new workers or disrupting a smooth-running system that was so personally profitable.

As a compromise, the SS decided Wiegleb could keep his crews, but they would live in Birkenau. Close to the camp's newest gas chambers.

With SS guards walking alongside, the prisoners marched out the main gate of Auschwitz and down the paved road to Birkenau. They marched through the gates of camp—and sank into ankle-deep mud.

Yet again, Rudi knew he'd descended even deeper into hell. This place was bigger than Auschwitz, a vast brown plain lined with dark wooden barracks. Skeletal prisoners lurched down unpaved paths. Overfed rats scurried between buildings. The air was rank with smoke and the stink of death.

On the western edge of camp stood four new red brick buildings, each with a tall chimney.

Like Rudi, Filip Müller was transferred to the Birkenau side of the Auschwitz complex. Unlike Rudi, Filip was forced to work *inside* the new brick buildings. He was one of the few prisoners to learn the secrets of these buildings and live to tell the story.

The first one he saw up close was Crematorium II. (The structure containing the complex's first gas chamber, Crematorium I, was back in the Auschwitz main camp.) Filip marched up with a Sonderkommando crew, passing through iron gates into a courtyard in front of a long brick building. Posted at the entrance, in several languages, were the words TO THE BATHS.

A set of steps led down to a doorway. The doorway opened on a cavernous room with low concrete ceilings and freshly whitewashed walls. There were signs on the room's support pillars:

CLEANLINESS BRINGS FREEDOM
ONE LOUSE MAY KILL YOU

Along the walls, about five feet off the ground, were wooden hooks, each one numbered, and wooden benches beneath the hooks. Signs instructed people to remember on which hook they had hung their clothing so that everything could be quickly retrieved after their shower.

Filip walked to the far end of the changing room. A passage, about fifteen feet long, led to another huge low-ceilinged chamber. Shower heads hung from the ceiling—another part of the deception. Deception even here, at the very end of the road.

Filip knew exactly what he was looking at. This was a gas chamber, much bigger than the one in the Auschwitz main camp. Big enough to kill a thousand people at a time.

Every detail had been carefully designed. Protective wire cages covered the light bulbs. There were structural pillars of concrete, as in the changing room, but also poles of thin metal, with small holes punched in the metal to let in the poison gas. A large fan mounted in the wall could be switched on to clear out the toxic air.

The architects had included an elevator to haul bodies up to the incinerator room on the first floor. Here Filip saw five new furnaces, each with three arched openings, and metal platforms on rollers leading to the oven doors.

Everything in this building was similar to what Filip had seen before, only bigger and newer, engineered to function like a factory. And this was just one of four such facilities in Birkenau.

"I began to fear," Filip would later say, "that what I had experienced so far was child's play to what awaited me."

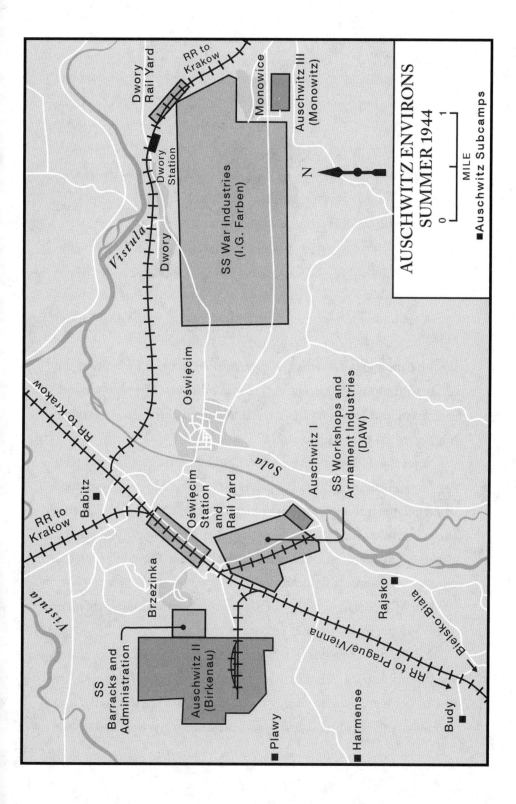

AUSCHWITZ ENVIRONS
SUMMER 1944

0   MILE   1
■ Auschwitz Subcamps

N

RR to Krakow
Dwory Rail Yard
Dwory Rail Yard
Dwory Station
Dwory
Vistula
Dwory
Oświęcim
Monowice
Auschwitz III
(Monowitz)
SS War Industries
(I.G. Farben)

Sola
Auschwitz I
SS Workshops and
Armament Industries
(DAW)

RR to Krakow
Babitz
Oświęcim Station
and Rail Yard
Brzezinka
Vistula
SS Barracks and
Administration
Auschwitz II
(Birkenau)
Plawy
Harmense
RR to Prague/Vienna
Rajsko
Bielsko-Biala
Budy

24

BY THE SPRING OF 1943, Gerta and her parents had survived a full year in hiding in Hungary.

"Somehow," she'd recall, "days that seemed endless in the beginning began to pass more quickly."

Since the German defeat at Stalingrad, Gerta's father was feeling hopeful about the war. A student of history, Max was reminded of Napoleon's invasion of Russia in 1812. The mighty French army made it all the way into Moscow before a combination of ferocious Russian resistance and a brutal Russian winter turned Napoleon's advance into a catastrophic retreat.

Could Hitler have made the same blunder with his Soviet invasion? Maybe. It was too soon to say.

Gerta, now sixteen, felt comfortable enough in her assumed identity to visit art galleries and go for long walks in Budapest. On one of her walks she met a boy her age, András. They shared a love of books and paintings, and began meeting for walks, sometimes holding hands. András read Gerta poems he'd written in his note-book.

Gerta enjoyed these romantic moments—yet could never really relax with her new friend. She carefully avoided conversations about politics, or the war, or her family. She couldn't even let the subject of school come up. How could she explain why she didn't go to school?

She was evasive at home as well. "When I was to meet him I just told my parents that I was going for a walk up the hill," Gerta later said. "I knew that they would worry that meeting András may be dangerous."

That summer, late one night, Gerta was startled by the sound of fists pounding on the family's apartment door.

It has to be the police, she thought. *Who else knocks like that?*

Jozefina opened the door. Two policemen strode in and demanded to see the family's identification. Max pulled their forged papers from a desk drawer. One of the officers studied the papers, unimpressed.

"You'd better come with us to the police station," he ordered. "We were told that you might be illegal immigrants. Pack a few personal things you want to take with you, because if your identity papers are not in order you will be sent to a detention camp."

Who had denounced them? Gerta suspected the building's con-cierge, that unpleasant man who watched the family come and go at odd hours, with no set routine.

Not András. She didn't want to believe it could be him.

Knowing they could be separated, Gerta and her parents packed separate bags. The despair on Max's face was painful to see. "I knew that the feeling of inadequacy swamped him," Gerta would recall. "He was unable to take proper care of us, and he couldn't bear it."

The police took all three of them to the station and quickly figured out that their papers were forged. The family spent ten days in a crowded Budapest prison. Then they were marched to the train station, loaded onto a boxcar with other prisoners, and shipped to the east.

After a year at Auschwitz, Rudi had learned that survival required a constant supply of willpower, resourcefulness, help from friends and strangers—and a lot of luck. It's hard to call Rudi's transfer to Birkenau lucky, but there was an aspect of luck to it. Because it was there, in Birkenau, that Rudi connected with Alfred Wetzler, a twenty-four-year-old Jewish prisoner from Rudi's hometown.

Fred had survived in camp even longer than Rudi. He'd managed to work his way into a coveted job: clerk in the Birkenau morgue.

Only here would this job be coveted. Fred sat at a desk in a dark wooden shed, surrounded by piles of corpses, men and women who had died of causes other than the gas chambers. He recorded the numbers tattooed on the prisoners' arms. He recorded the number of teeth with gold fillings that specially trained crews yanked with pliers from the mouths of the dead. The gold went into a tin can, which was collected at regular intervals by an SS guard.

On the plus side, the SS mostly left Fred alone—they didn't care for the smell in the shed. He was able to organize decent clothing and food for himself, and even served visitors something resembling coffee.

"How nice to see you!" Fred called out when he recognized Rudi. "Come in and make yourself at home!"

Fred was just as Rudi remembered. Thinner of course, but not starving, with quick humor and intelligent, smiling eyes. They hadn't been friends before the war; Fred had seemed so much older than Rudi back then. Here they bonded quickly.

Whenever he had a spare moment, Rudi ducked into the shed. He and Fred sat together and drank fake coffee. They talked about Trnava and shared memories of mutual friends.

They talked about ideas for escape.

The fact that the SS relied on prisoner labor gave prisoners such as Fred Wetzler, who did his job efficiently, a tiny amount of protection and influence. Fred used his connections with guards to get Rudi a new job as a barracks registrar—a sort of clerk and messenger—in the quarantine block of Birkenau, where new arrivals were held until they were assigned to work details. This was a privileged position, with incredible luxuries such as better food and real clothes in place of striped pajamas.

More important to Rudi, his daily tasks required him to walk around camp, giving him the chance to talk with prisoners as they arrived—the few who'd been selected for forced labor. Rudi asked for details of how many people they'd arrived with and where they were from, adding these facts to the ledger in his head.

Rudi's relative freedom of movement also allowed him to reconnect with Filip Müller. A lot of prisoners shunned members of the Sonderkommando, refused even to shake their hands, and Rudi got it, felt a bit of that disgust himself. What would he have done if ordered to work in the crematorium? He didn't think he'd do it.

Then again, who could say? Everyone was just trying to live through one more day.

Unless you've been faced with the decision—do this or die right now—you can't possibly know how you would respond.

Rudi and Filip met briefly when they could. Filip described what happened inside the new brick crematorium buildings. His main job was to keep the incinerator fires burning, though some days he was assigned to work in the changing room. These different jobs allowed him to see the Nazis' entire process at work. Murder on an industrial scale.

Again and again, Filip witnessed heartbreaking acts of dignity and courage. Groups of people singing together when they saw the end was near. Parents holding children, reassuring them. Women shouting at the SS: "Hitler will lose the war! Then will come the hour of revenge!"

In the undressing room, he saw a young woman whip off her shoe and slam its high heel into an SS man's forehead. When the guard reached up to cover the bloody gash in his face, the woman dove for his holster, grabbed his pistol, and shot him dead. The SS dealt with such disturbances by mounting machine guns in the changing room doorway and firing into the crowd.

Rudi added Filip's stories to the information he was collecting. All this evidence *had* to reach the outside world. But nothing could be written down. Rudi could be searched at any time. Everything was committed to memory.

It would have been much safer for Rudi to keep to himself, to ask no questions, to avoid any action that could draw the attention of kapos or the SS. With his new registrar position, he now had a decent chance to survive until the end of the war.

But that was not his only goal.

25

IN SPITE OF THE PRESSURE from Adolf Hitler, the Hungarian government had still not agreed to hand over the country's Jewish population.

"As regards the Jewish problem," Hungary's head of state, Miklós Horthy, wrote in a letter during the war, "I have been an anti-Semite through all my life." Yet Horthy did not think uprooting nearly a tenth of the population could be done without disrupting the country's economy. It simply wasn't in Hungary's best interests. This irritated Hitler, but there was little he could do—short of occupying the country.

So when Gerta and her parents were arrested and exposed as Jews, they were not shipped to a Nazi concentration camp. Instead, they were locked in a detention camp for illegal immigrants and political prisoners, a fenced-in compound on a hot, treeless plain in eastern Hungary.

Men and women were separated. Gerta and Jozefina were put in a flea-infested room with eight other women while Max was sent to the other side of camp. Gerta's mother made friends, even organized card games at night. Her father did not adapt as well.

"I really let you down, Gerti," Max said when they were able to meet briefly during the day. "I wish I could have protected you."

Gerta did not agree that he'd failed the family, not at all—but she knew her father. She understood his thinking. He was a gentle man who'd always been an optimist, who believed good things happened when you worked hard and followed the rules. The world he knew was shattered. He was losing his will to fight back.

In the evenings, as the summer air cooled, Gerta sat outside with a small group of Jewish girls who'd come to Hungary from Slovakia, Poland, and Croatia. The other teens had all been separated from their parents and told harrowing stories of life on the run. Gerta felt relatively sheltered. She had her parents with her. She had Hungarian relatives with good jobs who were probably working to get her out of this camp.

But how long, Gerta wondered, could she count on other people to save her?

"Perhaps I knew," she'd say, looking back at this moment, "that I should start learning how to face adverse situations independently and make my own decisions."

"You're like me," the Russian prisoner told Rudi. "You're going to get out or die like a soldier."

Dmitri Volkov. A tall, powerfully built Soviet soldier who'd been captured in battle and shipped to Sachsenhausen, near Berlin. He'd managed to escape and had made it all the way back to Kiev, nearly a thousand miles. He was almost out of German-held territory when he was recaptured. As punishment for escaping, the Nazis had sent him to Auschwitz.

Rudi struck up conversations with the older prisoner, at first just hoping to practice his Russian. They talked of great Russian authors, of Tolstoy and Dostoyevsky. As they grew to like and trust each other, they moved on to other subjects. "And now," Dmitri told Rudi in one of their talks, "I'm going to teach you some lessons."

Rudi pictured himself back home in the family living room, studying Russian while his mother cooked dinner. He remembered how she'd teased him about it.

What's a Jewish kid from Slovakia ever going to do with Russian?

"Lesson one is this," Dmitri said. "Trust nobody. Don't tell me, for instance, when you're going to escape or how." Dmitri didn't think he'd talk under torture, but how could he be sure?

"Lesson two," he continued. "Don't be afraid of the Germans. There are many of them, but each of them is small." They try to break your will in Auschwitz, he explained, and it works with many prisoners. But they can be killed as easily as anyone—this Dmitri knew from his own experience in battle.

"Lesson three: Once you're out, don't trust your legs because a bullet can always run faster." Dmitri had made a careless mistake in Kiev, charging too eagerly through a row of bushes—right into a German soldier who was in there with a woman. Rotten luck, but avoidable. "Be invisible," Dmitri told Rudi. The Polish territory outside Auschwitz was crawling with German soldiers. Rudi would have to hide when the sun was up, sleep by day, and travel only by night.

Lesson four: "Carry no money." A baffling bit of advice. It was easy enough to organize cash in camp. Wouldn't Rudi need it to buy food? No, Dmitri explained, that's exactly what you must not do. Rudi would be desperate for food; that was inevitable. If he had money in his pocket, he'd be tempted to slip into a village store. It would be impossible to go unnoticed in Nazi-occupied Poland—a stranger with a shaved head and a Slovak accent. Better to starve for a few days.

Lesson five: "Travel light." You'll need a knife, Dmitri advised, so you'll be ready to fight to the death at any moment. You'll need matches, to cook any food you're able to forage, and a watch, which can be used as a compass. Dmitri explained the process: Hold the watch face flat on your palm. Angle it so the hour hand points in the direction of the sun. Note the midpoint between the hour hand and the twelve o'clock position on the watch dial: in the northern hemisphere that midpoint is south, roughly.

"Never forget that the fight only begins when you're away from the camp," Dmitri said. "We'd better not meet again because we have been seen talking together too much already."

By the end of fall 1943, the SS had dismantled the killing centers of Belzec, Treblinka, and Sobibor. This was partly due to acts of resistance by the prisoners.

At Treblinka, as at other camps, a small number of Jewish men and women were kept alive as forced labor. That summer, a group of prisoners stole weapons from the guards' arsenal, lit the camp's wooden buildings on fire, and charged through the main gate as guards fired from watchtowers. More than three hundred prisoners made it into the surrounding forest, although two-thirds of them were eventually captured and killed.

In October, prisoners at Sobibor pulled off a more elaborate revolt. On the chosen day, a prisoner who worked in the tailor shop invited an SS guard in to be fitted for a new uniform. The guard took off his belt, with its holster and pistol, and tried on a jacket. As one prisoner checked the fit, another stepped up and killed the guard with an axe. The rebels grabbed the gun and tossed the body in the corner. Minutes later, another guard entered the cobbler shop to pick up a pair of boots—and got the same treatment.

At a signal from the leader of the revolt, several hundred prisoners made a break for the main gate or barbed wire fences. Of the three hundred who made it to the woods, about a hundred were caught in the following days. About fifty survived the war by joining partisan groups or hiding with sympathetic Polish farmers. The stories of what they'd seen in Nazi death camps would not become public until the fighting was over.

Himmler ordered Sobibor destroyed. He ordered the gas chamber demolished, the buildings dynamited. Nazi crews plowed over Sobibor, as well as Belzec and Treblinka, planting trees to conceal evidence of what had happened there.

To Himmler, in spite of the revolts, these camps had been a success. Most of Poland's Jewish population had been deported and gassed. More than 1.5 million people were murdered in these three camps—mostly Jews, but also non-Jewish Poles, Roma, and Soviet prisoners of war. "This is a page of glory in our history which has never been written, and is never to be written," Himmler said in a speech to senior SS officers in October 1943.

Meanwhile, Hitler's "Final Solution" would continue. Auschwitz was still in operation. This is where the job was to be finished.

26

GERTA AND HER PARENTS WERE released after a month in the Hungarian detention camp. This was thanks to one of Gerta's uncles, Arthur, who paid enormous bribes to government officials.

The family returned to Budapest, where Gerta could feel the war closing in. People in the street spoke of their fear of Allied air raids. Windows were covered at night, hiding the city's lights from enemy bombers. Hitler was steadily increasing his economic demands on Hungary, taking more and more from the country's farms and factories. Shortages worsened as winter set in, and Gerta and her mother took turns bundling up and standing in line for hours, hoping for the chance to buy a loaf of bread or a hunk of cheese.

Seventeen now, and desperate to do something active and helpful, Gerta arranged a job working for a distant cousin, a woman nicknamed Baby who wanted a nanny for her three small children. Gerta moved into Baby's home in the hills above town, a luxurious villa with grand views of the city and the Danube River. It all felt slightly unreal, as if floating over the troubles of the world.

But Gerta no longer had any illusions about the future. She overheard Baby making arrangements with non-Jewish friends to hide herself and her children when the time came. Gerta knew she'd soon need a new plan too.

Rudi Vrba had survived more than a year and a half in Auschwitz. In the jargon of the camp, there were "new" prisoners and "old" prisoners. Rudi was an ancient prisoner.

He was nineteen.

In January 1944, as he hurried between buildings with a notebook under his arm, Rudi watched work crews begin a new project along the road between the front gates of Birkenau and two of the new crematorium buildings. He later spoke to one of the men he'd seen working on the project, a Polish kapo he knew well enough to ask a discreet question.

They were building a railway line, the kapo told him. A short spur, a bit over a mile of track, connecting the main line into Auschwitz with the new buildings in Birkenau.

What for? Rudi asked.

Kapos were not privy to such information. But the man had heard a few SS guards joking about how "good times are coming." They were excited about the new goods that would soon be arriving from Hungary. They specifically said Hungary.

Rudi gathered an additional clue from Filip Müller. Filip let Rudi know that crews were digging pits for mass graves, adding capacity to destroy bodies even beyond that of the four crematoria in Birkenau.

In the morgue, Rudi talked this over with Fred Wetzler. Both Rudi and Fred were sometimes able to organize newspapers, giving guards cash found among prisoners' possessions for quick looks at the news. German troops were retreating in the Soviet Union, but still far from defeated. Hungary, with its large Jewish population, had not yet fallen under Hitler's control. Was that about to change?

This is the moment, Rudi thought. *The escape has to be soon.*

Escape—but how?

Lots of prisoners thought they'd found the answer.

One was a Slovak named Fero Langer, a big guy, boisterous and always laughing, always willing to share his bread. Rudi had first met Fero in the Nováky transport camp in Slovakia, a lifetime ago. Now, early in 1944, the Nazis dumped Fero in Birkenau. He immediately devised a plan to get out.

"I've just met a very interesting fellow," Fero told Rudi. "An SS man."

The man was named Dobrovolny, Fero explained. He'd grown up in Slovakia. Fero had gone to school with him; they'd sat next to each other in class; they'd been good pals, like brothers!

Rudi shared Dmitri's advice: Trust nobody. Especially not a Nazi.

Sure, sure, Fero knew that. But Dobrovolny was different. Fero had given him letters to deliver to the outside world. Dobrovolny had taken the letters with him when he went home on leave, and he'd even brought the replies to Fero.

Fero had it all worked out. He knew people on the outside who could get him large sums of money. In exchange for a huge payment, Dobrovolny would buy a truck and park it in the woods near camp. He'd arrange to get Fero, and a few select prisoners, assigned to a work party under his supervision. Dobrovolny would march the men out of camp for what would look like a routine job. They'd get in the truck and drive off, shooting any SS men who got in their way.

Fero wanted to bring along four other prisoners, each from a different country. This would make it easier for them to quickly spread the word of what was happening in Auschwitz.

Rudi hoped it would work. But he had a bad feeling about it.

Later that week, around three in the afternoon, the siren wailed. The escape siren.

Guards started running around camp, shouting to each other, leading dogs on leashes. The search was on. Rudi felt a surge of optimism. Fero would pull it off, if anyone could.

Three hours passed. Rudi pictured Fero and his crew in their truck, the towns they were passing on their way south. He pictured Fero ditching the truck on the side of the road, darting into the forest along the border, crossing into Slovakia on foot.

None of that happened.

The Nazis brought back five dead prisoners that evening—Fero and his four recruits. Guards put the bodies on display in the middle of camp.

Filip Müller was walking back from the crematorium when he saw the gory exhibit. Three bodies lay in the dirt. Two more sat on stools, propped against the handles of shovels. The two on the stools were Fero Langer and a man Filip knew well, a French Jew, Daniel Obstbaum, who had the bunk next to his. A friend.

The dead men's eyes were wide open. Their shirts ripped apart and soaked with blood. Between Fero and Daniel was a message scrawled on a wooden board: "Three cheers, we've come back again!"

Dobrovolny, it turned out, had informed on Fero the moment Fero suggested his plan. The SS ambushed Fero and the others as soon as they left camp. Dobrovolny got a week's leave as a reward, and the SS got five bullet-riddled bodies to put on display. A blunt force message meant to crush all hope of escape.

It didn't work. Rudi continued searching for a plan.

27

"YOU AND I ARE GOING to get out of this bloody camp soon," Charles Unglick told Rudi one night when they were sitting together in Charles's room in his barracks. "We're going to go to Paris and live it up."

Charles—"Charlo" to friends like Rudi—was a Polish-born Jew who'd emigrated with his parents to France. He'd become a captain in the French army and was captured by the Germans in 1940. Charlo was a block senior in Birkenau and a master organizer—food and clothes for himself, and cash and luxuries he used to bribe guards. There was one particular SS man Charlo was sure would help him get away.

The plan sounded similar to Fero's. This SS man Charlo was cultivating worked as a delivery driver in camp. At an agreed-upon time, he'd park his truck in Charlo's block, open the back, and start unloading wood. That was all routine. And it was normal for the driver to haul around a huge tool chest in the back of the truck. On the chosen day, he'd leave the chest unlocked. When his back was turned, Charlo and Rudi would jump into the truck and shut themselves in the chest. The driver would lock it before he drove away. If guards at the front gate asked to see into the chest, the driver would simply say that he'd forgotten his key and that the thing had been locked since he'd picked up the truck that morning.

Again, Rudi thought of Dmitri's warning. Never trust a Nazi.

This was no normal Nazi, Charlo explained. This guy had been orphaned as a young kid in Romania and brought up by Jewish parents, speaking Yiddish and everything! He'd joined the SS when the Germans occupied Romania, mainly as a way to survive, and didn't buy into their antisemitic nonsense.

Rudi was unconvinced. So the man spoke Yiddish, fine. He wore a Nazi uniform now. He must be expecting more than the gratitude of a couple of Jewish prisoners.

A lot more, Charlo explained. Through his contacts in the Sonderkommando, Charlo was organizing a fortune in gold and diamonds. That would seal the deal.

"We'll be out by the end of the week," he told Rudi. "I don't know exactly when we go, but our friend will tell us."

Rudi had thought about escape for so long. He knew he'd get only one try. Was this it—the best opportunity he'd ever have?

How was he supposed to know?

He told Charlo he was in.

A few tense days passed. Rudi knew not to ask for updates; his friend would tell him when it was time. He was in the latrine when Charlo came in, wearing a new leather belt. Rudi jokingly asked if he could have it.

"You bastard!" Charlo said, laughing. "I tell you what—you can have it when I die."

Then, lowering his voice to a whisper, Charlo added: "Our car leaves in three days' time at seven o'clock after roll call. Don't be late."

Three days later, on the evening of January 25, 1944, Rudi's block was dismissed from roll call at 6:45.

He paced outside Charlo's barracks, hardly able to believe the Nazis had made him line up for the last time. Trying to appear relaxed, Rudi chatted with other prisoners. He didn't hear a word they were saying.

No sign of Charlo yet. No delivery truck. It was seven o'clock.

Rudi forced himself to keep walking back and forth. Another five minutes passed. The SS driver had informed on them—that must be it. Otherwise, where was the truck? Another five minutes passed.

"Rudi!"

Startled, he spun around. Not Charlo. Another prisoner, a man from Rudi's barracks. The man was laughing at Rudi for jumping like a frightened cat.

"Sorry," Rudi said. "Did you want something?"

Just a message, the man said. Dr. Andrej Milar, a friend from their barracks, had organized a pot of goulash soup and Rudi was welcome to a bowl.

"Tell him . . . ," Rudi began, hesitating as he realized how ridiculous this was going to sound. "Tell him I'm not hungry."

The man walked away, amazed.

7:15. Still no Charlo. No delivery truck. It must not be coming tonight, Rudi figured.

Knowing he couldn't stand around forever without drawing attention, he walked back to his barracks and went inside to eat some soup. He'd just finished, and was heading back outside, when a prisoner ran up and told him Charles Unglick was looking for him.

"Have they brought the wood to his block yet?" Rudi asked.

Yes, the man said. They were unloading it now.

Rudi sprinted back to Charlo's barracks. The wood was there. The truck was gone.

He ran into Charlo's room. Empty. He dropped to his knees and pried up a floorboard under which he'd seen Charlo hide his treasures. Empty.

Rudi was furious with himself, physically sick at the thought he'd traded his one shot at freedom for a lousy bowl of soup.

Actually, the soup saved him.

The SS driver brought Charlo's lifeless body back to camp later that evening. The guards propped him on a stool, held up by shovels. They left him on display for two days.

The story that spread through camp was that the SS driver had driven straight to a garage, opened the tool chest, and shot Charlo. No word of the gold and diamonds Charlo had had on him, but Rudi could guess where those wound up.

He felt a conflicting mix of emotions. Fury and sadness, but also relief. Selfish relief. That could have been him in that tool chest. Anyway, he was not about to give up. It didn't matter how many others failed. He was going to get out.

When a crew came to take Charlo to the crematorium, friends washed his body and wrapped him in a blanket. They split up his clothes.

"What do you want?" someone asked Rudi. "The boots?"

"I want the belt," Rudi said. "Just the belt."

No one could believe it. Rudi was Charlo's good friend. He should take whatever he wanted. If not the boots, at least the sweater.

Rudi picked up the leather belt and strapped it around his narrow waist.

By March 1944, the tide of the war had clearly turned against Adolf Hitler. The Red Army was advancing in the east, driving German forces back toward Poland. Allied bombers were devastating Berlin and other German cities. But the Germans were still fighting.

In mid-March, Hitler ordered his troops into Hungary.

Miklós Horthy stayed on in the role of regent, but with greatly reduced day-to-day power over the government. Units of the SS and the Gestapo—Hitler's massive secret police force—began the process of isolating Hungary's Jewish population. Jews were ordered to give up their telephones, radios, cars, even their bicycles.

"We knew our days in Budapest were numbered," Gerta later said.

Her father was in the most immediate danger. As a condition of the family's release from the detention camp, Max was required to report to the Budapest police on the first day of every month.

In a terrifying way, news of the German occupation of Hungary fit with everything Rudi had seen over the last few months. It explained the new rail line directly to the crematoria and the new mass graves he'd learned about from Filip. The Nazis were expanding their death factory, planning to kill even faster. Win or lose the war, Hitler intended to finish what he had begun.

At first, Rudi had wanted to escape to save his own life. Then he'd wanted to escape to tell the world what he'd seen. That was all still true, but now he had an even more pressing need to get out. Lives could be saved—maybe hundreds of thousands of lives—if someone could get out and sound the alarm.

Of course, no amount of added motivation would make it any easier to escape from Auschwitz.

But this time was different. This time Rudi had a plan.

PART III
ESCAPE

28

IT BEGAN WITH ONE SIMPLE but surprising idea: To get out of Auschwitz, you'd have to escape—and then hide *inside* the camp.

By the spring of 1944, Rudi Vrba had seen most corners of the enormous Auschwitz-Birkenau complex. He understood exactly how it was defended. Birkenau, like the Auschwitz main camp, was surrounded by electrified barbed wire fences. The camp was ringed with watchtowers, giving guards a clear view of everything. This was the inner perimeter of defense.

There was also an outer perimeter. A second layer of watchtowers formed a giant ring around Auschwitz-Birkenau, including the warehouses and railroad ramp. The territory between the inner and outer perimeters was flat and open, with no place to hide.

But not all watchtowers of the inner and outer perimeters were manned all the time. This was the weakness—if circumstances were just right.

Prisoners were counted each morning, then marched to work at sites outside the inner perimeter but inside the outer perimeter.

Guards kept watch from the outer towers all day. Anyone attempting to approach the outer fence was an easy target.

At night, the prisoners marched back inside the inner perimeter. They were counted again. When the SS confirmed that no one was missing, the guards came down from the outer towers. There was no need for them at night because everyone was already inside the inner perimeter, which was heavily guarded by soldiers in watchtowers with bright lights and machine guns. Early in the morning, guards returned to the outer watchtowers. The prisoners were counted and marched to work.

What if someone was missing at roll call? There was a system for that, too.

If a prisoner was missing, the outer ring of guards stayed in place while SS teams with specially trained dogs searched every inch of the camp. The search continued for three days, with the outer perimeter guarded at all times.

If the prisoner was not found in three days, it was presumed they were dead somewhere, lost in a pile of bodies. Just in case they'd actually gotten out, Nazi authorities outside the camp would be alerted of the possible escape. And things in Auschwitz went back to normal, with the guards in the outer watchtowers leaving their posts at night.

Those three days were the key.

Was it possible to remain hidden *outside* the inner perimeter but *inside* the outer perimeter for three days?

Maybe, maybe not. But say you could. Then you could wait for the third night. Wait for the Nazis to remove the outer guard, slip out of your hiding place in the dark, and go under the wires.

The only thing missing was a hiding place. And the Nazis provided that themselves.

Nazi authorities were expanding Auschwitz-Birkenau again in the spring of 1944, racing to build a new set of barracks on the Birkenau side of the complex in preparation for the expected transports from Hungary. Huge piles of lumber sat in the dirt of this construction site, an area of camp prisoners dubbed "Mexico."

In their haste to enslave and kill more people, the Nazis provided Rudi with his first real chance to escape.

He was not the only one to see the potential. Rudi's friend Fred Wetzler told him that four Jewish prisoners on the mortuary crew were going to make a break for it. They needed Fred and Rudi's help.

"You know the planks they've stacked for the new camp they're building?" Fred asked.

Rudi nodded.

Well, the mortuary crew had bribed a few kapos who worked at the construction site, Fred explained. The kapos had piled one stack of lumber with a cavity under the wood, a space big enough for four men to hide.

Genius. The construction site was outside the inner fences of Birkenau, but inside the camp's outer security perimeter. If the men could hide there for seventy-two hours, they should be able to sneak through the outer perimeter at night.

"How can we help?" Rudi asked.

"All they want us to do is keep them posted about what's happening in the camp while they're hiding."

Rudi was glad to agree. Maybe these guys would be the ones to finally succeed, to get out and sound the alarm.

A few days later, after evening roll call, the sirens blared. Four prisoners from the mortuary were missing.

As a registrar, Rudi was expected to move around camp, delivering papers and messages between different sections. This gave him an up-front look at the massive search—more than a thousand SS men, Rudi estimated, with a couple hundred dogs, scouring and sniffing every corner of the outer camp.

When there were no guards near the lumber pile, Rudi walked past holding a stack of papers, reading as he walked.

"They're over by the crematoria now," Rudi said, stopping as if to study his papers. "They've been past here a dozen times, but they've never even looked at the wood."

A faint response came through the layers of lumber: "O.K. Thanks."

For three days, Rudi and Fred took turns whispering updates to the men in the pile. After seventy-two hours, the Nazis gave up the search.

Rudi walked past the planks on the fourth day and whispered a message.

No answer. *They were free!*

But not free. They were in Nazi-occupied Poland. The Gestapo would be hunting for them everywhere.

Still, they were out of Auschwitz, clear of the first obstacle. Best of all, the hiding place had not been discovered. It could be used again. Rudi and Fred agreed to give it some time, let things drift back to normal in camp.

In two weeks, they would go into the wood pile.

* * *

One week later, the four men from the mortuary marched back into camp, cut up and badly bruised, closely guarded by smirking SS men.

Rudi had long since lost count of the low points. The devastating blows. The times he'd thought it couldn't get worse. This was a new depth of misery. Not only had the men failed to alert the world of Nazi plans, but they'd clearly been beaten, tortured for information on how they'd escaped. Rudi's only chance to get out was gone.

Or was it?

As the guards marched their prisoners past the spot where Rudi stood, one of them, a Slovak man named Sandor Eisenbach, looked at Rudi and winked.

29

A WINK. A QUICK DROP of an eyelid.

What did that mean?

Rudi and Fred went over and over the question. Their hopeful interpretation: Sandor was passing a message. He hadn't talked. The secret hiding place was still good.

But the violent interrogations would certainly continue. Wouldn't one of the men eventually crack?

That's what Rudi expected. The prisoners would be forced to talk and then hanged on the gallows the SS rolled out for escape attempts. Rudi found out the men had been taken to the dreaded Block 11 of Auschwitz, the punishment block. He invented an errand for himself and talked his way past the guards into the walled-in courtyard beside the brick building.

Sandor Eisenbach and the others were there, kneeling in the dirt, digging a hole with their bare hands. The work served no purpose other than torture.

Rudi stepped close to Sandor and whispered, "Do they know about it?"

Sandor dumped a handful of loose earth into his cap. "No," he said.

"Are you sure?"

"I swear it." Sandor never looked up from the ditch.

Rudi reported the news to Fred. They agreed that Sandor was absolutely trustworthy.

The next day, hoping to learn what had gone wrong, Rudi risked another quick conversation with Sandor in Block 11.

"We ran into a military patrol outside Porąbka," Sandor said.

Rudi still had the map in his head, the image from the children's atlas he'd studied in the latrine. He could picture the spot. A town on the Sola River, about halfway between Auschwitz and the Slovak border.

"Steer clear of that place," Sandor warned. "Not much of a town, but it's stinking with soldiers."

There was one other thing, he said. When they were hiding in the lumber, the prisoners carved a little message to the Nazis on the wood and signed it with their prisoner numbers. A foolish impulse that could only make their situation worse.

Rudi promised to scratch out the message.

A day before he was due to report to the police in Budapest, Gerta's father came for a visit at Baby's house in the hills above town.

This was a scene Gerta would relive again and again in years to come. Max walked into her small room. She suggested a walk in the sunshine, but he was in no mood to enjoy the day. He slumped on the bed and looked at her. She saw love in his expression, and suffering.

"You must forgive me," he said. "I have always made the wrong decisions."

From the start of their flight, Max had blamed himself for not being able to protect his family. It wasn't fair or logical, but Gerta understood; it was how he felt. Had he come to say goodbye? The misery on his face made her think so, though she tried not to believe it.

She kissed him. She told him what a wonderful father he was.

"Gerti," he said, beginning to cry, "please remember all the good times we had together."

He stood and hugged her.

Max walked into a police station in Budapest on April 1, 1944. Doing as he was told, he hoped, would help keep his wife and daughter safe.

A few days later, a man knocked on the door of the family apartment and spoke with Jozefina. The man had been in prison with Max and brought a message from him: the police would soon be coming for the rest of the family. Jozefina and Gerta must go into hiding immediately.

Jozefina got word to Gerta, who threw her things into a bag and said goodbye to Baby.

"This war will end soon," Baby said, "and then we will all get together again."

A nice thought. To Gerta, it did not sound very realistic.

Rudi and Fred were nearly ready to make their attempt.

They arranged for two Polish prisoners who worked in the mortuary, men they trusted, to replace the wooden planks over their heads after they'd climbed into the lumber pile. Through friends in Canada Command, they organized decent suits and overcoats, good leather boots, watches, matches, and knives. Following another one of Dmitri's instructions, they soaked tobacco in gasoline and let it dry.

The only other thing they planned to bring was information. Detailed descriptions of every aspect of the Auschwitz operation, in particular the gas chambers. It would have been much safer not to gather such evidence—any question or conversation could easily be overheard. But Rudi and Fred were not doing this for themselves.

Their biggest source of forbidden knowledge was Filip Müller.

Filip described the entire process in detail. He explained that thirty minutes after the gas chamber doors were bolted shut, the SS turned on ventilation fans. The doors were opened and members of the Sonderkommando, wearing gas masks, had the horrific job of untangling bodies and dragging them to the elevator.

The goal was theft as well as murder. Teeth with gold fillings were yanked out and sent to a special workshop. The Nazis dissolved the teeth in acid, melted the gold into bars, and sent them on to Berlin. Jewelry and eyeglasses were taken from the corpses, and women's hair was cut off, washed, and sent to factories to make industrial threads. To destroy the evidence of genocide, ashes from the ovens were dumped into local ponds and rivers.

Rudi and Fred committed all this to memory. They finalized the time and date for their attempt: April 3, at 2:00 p.m. Two days away.

They tried not to think about all the things that could still go wrong.

30

ON APRIL 3, A FEW minutes before 2:00 p.m., Rudi approached the SS man guarding the gate of the quarantine block. Rudi was wearing a suit and overcoat, but this was not so unusual; registrars were able to organize decent clothing. He told the guard he needed to go to one of the crematorium buildings on an errand. This too was routine and did not raise eyebrows.

"Bring me back a pair of socks," the SS man told him.

Rudi slipped out to the construction area. The two Polish prisoners were there. No sign of Fred.

Rudi and the Poles knew better than to hang around. All three turned around and went back to their normal duties. Rudi told the guard at the gate of his block that he'd forgotten the socks.

That night, Fred told Rudi there'd been an especially vicious SS man at the gate of his block. He'd decided not to risk lying to the man about needing to leave the mortuary.

They tried again the next day. The SS guard in Rudi's block

reminded him about the socks. This time Fred made it to the wood pile, but one of the Polish prisoners never showed—he'd been sent on some other errand by a kapo.

Small things went wrong each of the next two days. Everyone drifted back to where they belonged. The guard at the quarantine block gate was out of patience.

"If you don't bring me back those socks," he told Rudi on the fifth day, "you needn't bother coming back at all!"

Rudi promised not to forget.

He was nearly to the lumber pile when two young SS officers, men he'd never seen before, grabbed him by his overcoat.

"What have we here?" one of them said, chuckling at Rudi's suit. "Have you ever seen anything like this tailor's dummy?"

They must be new to camp, Rudi realized. The outfit wouldn't stand out to more experienced guards.

"I wonder," the other officer said, "what the gentleman has in his fine pockets?"

Rudi had a watch inside his shirt. A knife in his pants pocket. Strictly forbidden items. He felt cold sweat drip down the small of his back.

One of the guards thrust his hand into a pocket of Rudi's overcoat and pulled out a handful of cigarettes. Rudi had grabbed them at the last moment, just to have for the journey.

"He must be a heavy smoker!" the young Nazi said. He opened his hand, letting the cigarettes fall into the mud.

Rudi was a dead man. He knew it. Next they'd search his shirt.

The guards smacked Rudi with their bamboo canes.

"I'll teach you to act the gentleman around here."

"I'll teach you to smuggle cigarettes!"

The two Poles from the mortuary walked past, pretending not to notice the Jew being beaten.

After a sharp blow to Rudi's face, one the SS men growled: "Now get back to your section before I break your neck!"

Rudi spun and raced away, back toward the quarantine block.

When he got behind the cover of a half-built barracks, Rudi stopped, turned, and took another route toward the lumber pile, trying to calm his steps into the casual stride of a routine errand.

The Polish prisoners stood on top of the stack of wood, shifting planks as if for some construction job. They looked surprised to see that Rudi had made it, but said nothing. Fred was there. The Poles moved a plank and nodded to Rudi and Fred.

The thought flashed through Rudi's mind: *Once we go in there, there's no turning back.*

He and Fred jumped onto the pile and dropped through a narrow opening between boards. They'd barely hit the ground when a plank slid over the gap above them, blocking most of the sunlight. More boards covered the hole, and the tiny chamber went dark and silent.

They crouched in the dirt, unable to stand in the tight space. Their eyes adjusted and they could see a little by the faint light seeping between the boards. Rudi was trying so hard to be quiet he'd almost stopped breathing. He checked his pocket to make sure the knife was there. No matter what, he was not going back alive.

It was fifteen minutes before Rudi could take a decent breath. He felt his muscles relax a tiny bit. He looked around at the sides of their wooden cave, and there it was. Sandor's message to the SS:

"Kiss our arses!"

Rudi shaved off the words with the edge of his knife. It helped to have something to do. He thought of the gasoline-soaked tobacco he'd stuffed into his pockets. Russian tobacco, in honor of Dmitri. This was the best way to throw off search dogs, Dmitri had said, the best way to cover the scent of humans. Working slowly, methodically, Rudi and Fred forced tobacco into the cracks between the planks of their walls and roof.

Then they sat on the cold ground, settling in for a long wait. Rudi forced his brain to cycle through a series of positive thoughts:

No more roll calls.

No more bowing to SS men.

Soon you'll be free!

Reality crept in. *Free—or dead.*

Hours passed. Days. Weeks. Rudi pulled out his watch and angled its face toward the dim light.

It was only 3:30. They'd been in the wood pile for barely an hour.

How was that possible?

The siren would sound at about 5:30. The search would begin. Rudi dreaded it, but wished it would come already. The waiting was worse.

He kept checking his watch, kept lifting it to his ear to make sure it was still ticking. He held back a laugh at the memory of standing impatiently at the stove of the family kitchen with his mother. "A watched pot never boils!" she always said.

Neither Rudi nor Fred had slept well for days leading up to the attempt. Now would be a good time to get some sleep, but that was impossible. What if the tobacco didn't work? What if the work crews decided to use this pile of wood?

They heard the distant clomp of wooden shoes on pavement. The faint music of the orchestra as groups of prisoners marched back from work. The shouts of kapos getting everyone into line for roll call.

Rudi checked the time. It was 5:25.

Then 5:30. The SS would discover they were missing at any moment. Still no siren.

5:45. No siren.

Rudi and Fred did not need words to communicate.

What's taking so long?

Has someone talked?

Do the Germans already know where we are?

It was six o'clock. The dim sunlight was fading. They heard voices in the distance, men speaking in German, but too far off to make out the words. Rudi squeezed the handle of his knife. Their little cave seemed to be shrinking. Rudi pictured his bloody body on a stool, Fred's beside his, propped up by shovels, a sign on their laps: BECAUSE THEY TRIED TO ESCAPE.

The siren cut off his thoughts. The screech rose to a piercing height and held there, then fell and rose again.

Rudi looked to his friend. There was just enough light to see the glow in Fred's eyes.

31

FILIP MÜLLER KNEW WHAT THE siren meant.

He watched teams of kapos and guards snap into action. They charged into every barracks, every storeroom and latrine. Teams of SS men, with their dogs, left the inner perimeter to search the outer camp. Many of them headed straight for Mexico, the construction area. Bright lights illuminated the inner and outer camps. Guards manned every watchtower.

The first night is the key, Filip thought. *Let them make it through this first night, and they'll have a chance.*

Rudi and Fred heard the shouts of hundreds of SS men. The roar of motorcycle engines, the thump of boots on dirt, the barking dogs. It sounded like chaos, but those men had a system.

And the voices were getting closer.

"Look behind those planks!" someone shouted in German.

Men jumped on the lumber pile, rattling the top of the hideout, sending down a blizzard of dust. Rudi and Fred clapped hands over their noses to hold back what would be a catastrophic sneeze. Boots hammered the roof of their cave, and there was a lighter sound, the scratch of the nails of dogs' feet. Between the guards' shouts, Rudi could hear the dogs panting and sniffing.

He had his blade out. So did Fred. They may be found, but they'd take a few Nazis down with them.

The search party moved on. Their shouts and curses faded, mixing in with other groups in the area.

A tiny victory. Fred allowed himself to smile.

Other searchers soon followed, climbing on top of the wood pile. This went on all night. Rudi and Fred had bread in their coat pockets but were too charged up to eat.

Late that night they heard the rumble of trucks on the road that ran between Mexico and the Birkenau main camp. Rudi tried to count the trucks. Fifty, maybe more. All headed to the gas chambers. Rudi could not help the people in those trucks. He could not help anyone until he got out of this place.

The friends nodded off at various points during that long first night, only to be startled awake by noises of the search. The damp of the earth soaked through their clothes, and they shivered with cold. Unable to move around, barely able to stretch, their limbs cramped and ached.

The next morning, after sunrise, they heard a voice they recognized. One of their Polish friends from the mortuary. He was singing.

Their agreed-upon signal. All was well.

The search for the missing prisoners continued all day. Rudi thought the voices of the guards sounded angrier now, even desperate. They'd looked everywhere and were going over the same ground again. At two that afternoon, Rudi and Fred passed the twenty-four-hour mark in the lumber pile. They still could not touch their food.

"Just a day and a half more," Fred whispered that evening. "By now they must be sure we're miles away."

It was the only logical explanation for their disappearance. That's what made the plan so brilliant.

The forty-eight-hour mark passed.

A bit later that afternoon, their third in the wood pile, Rudi and Fred heard voices talking in German. Prisoners, not SS men.

"They can't have got away," one of the prisoners said. "They must be in the camp still."

The men traded theories about possible hiding places.

"How about that pile of wood?"

"The dogs have been over it a dozen times."

Then came the unmistakable thunder of shoes on the pile. The men started moving planks, lifting and dropping them, no doubt fantasizing about the reward they'd get from the SS if they solved the mystery.

Rudi and Fred crouched with their backs to the walls of their cave, knives out.

Someone shouted. Not the men on the lumber pile—this came from far away. There were more shouts, and running footsteps.

One of the men on the pile said, "They've got them!"

The men jumped down and ran off to investigate the commotion. They did not come back.

The last night and day were comparatively quiet. The SS crews were still out there, still searching, but with less haste, less shouting. The seventy-two-hour mark passed. In just a few hours, prisoners would march back from work and line up for evening roll call. The guards would come down from the outer watchtowers, darkness would fall . . .

Minutes crawled by that afternoon. If Rudi hadn't heard the ticking of his watch, he'd have been sure it had stopped.

Finally, he heard the orchestra playing, the groups marching back to the inner camp. The roll call began—another make-or-break moment for the escape. What if someone was missing from the count? What if the escape siren began to wail? The search would begin all over. Three more days, three more nights . . .

"Vacate guard posts!"

Had Rudi and Fred heard that right? The shout sounded far off.

But the command was repeated, a little louder this time. "Vacate guard posts!"

Still louder: "Vacate guard posts!"

Then softer, more distant: "Vacate guard posts!"

The guards in the outer watchtowers were calling to each other, passing on the command to stand down. Minutes later, a few of them walked past the wood pile, chatting on their way back to the center of camp.

Then nothing. Just the distant sounds, from about five hundred yards away, of a normal night in Birkenau.

"It could be a trick," Rudi whispered.

Fred agreed. Let it get later. Let it get darker.

The last of the sunlight faded and was replaced by the glow of lights on the inner watchtowers.

At nine they got to their feet, biting back howls of agony as they straightened their legs. Weak from hunger and thirst, they lifted their hands to a plank of their roof and pushed.

It wouldn't move.

They pushed harder, digging their boots into the earth, their stiff joints screaming, slivers from the rough plank slicing their hands. But the thing would not budge.

Both men were suddenly sweating, fighting panic. The weight of the wood to their cramped, exhausted bodies—that was the one factor they had not considered.

Time sped up now. If they couldn't get out that night, they'd have to wait another twenty-four hours. And they'd only grow weaker as time passed.

Rudi and Fred looked at each other, again communicating without words.

They reached up to the wood. Working together, grunting and sweating, with a combination of brute force and ferocious willpower, they shoved the board a few inches to one side.

They listened for sounds from outside but could hear nothing over their own gasps for air.

Looking up, between planks of wood, they saw a narrow wedge of starry black sky.

32

WHAT WOULD HAVE HAPPENED IF those German prisoners hadn't climbed onto the pile to search for the missing Jews? What if they hadn't slid a few of the boards aside, lightening the roof over Fred and Rudi's cave?

No time to ponder that now.

They widened the opening. Rudi locked his hands. Fred placed a boot on Rudi's palms. Fred got his elbows on top of the timber and wriggled up and out of the hole. Rudi pushed loose earth into a mound, giving himself a few extra inches, then reached up and gripped the edges of the wood and lifted himself, with Fred yanking on his overcoat from above.

From the top of the lumber pile they looked toward the inner camp, a view they'd never seen at night from the outside. Bright lights shone along the electrified fences. Searchlights swept the barracks from tall watchtowers.

The other direction, toward the outer perimeter, was dark. They could just make out the distant silhouettes of empty guard towers, about half a mile away.

Rudi and Fred slid the planks back over the hole in the pile. Maybe, if all went well, someone else could use the hiding spot. They dropped to the dirt and listened. All quiet.

On elbows and knees, as flat to the cold ground as they could get, they slithered toward a gap between watchtowers.

When they made it to the outer fence, Fred eased a stick under the lowest wire and stood it upright, lifting the wire. They slid under the fence and pulled out the stick, leaving behind as few clues as possible.

In front of them was a small stand of birch trees. They crawled toward it.

When they reached the cover of the woods they stood up and, stooping at first, began to run.

The fight only begins when you're away from the camp.

Dmitri's words ran through Rudi's mind. The small miracle he and Fred had just pulled off was worthless on its own. The real struggle was just beginning.

They came to the edge of the woods and looked out on open grassland dotted with low shrubs. They fell to their bellies and crawled. The ground out here was soft and muddy, not packed down by guards' boots, and they sloshed through freezing puddles, arcing around the north edge of the camp toward the Vistula River.

Rumor was that the SS had laid land mines in these fields. But there was nothing Rudi and Fred could do to defend themselves against this danger, no sense in slowing down. They crawled past signs on wooden posts here and there—warnings of the mines maybe? Didn't matter. It was too dark to read signs.

They stopped and lay still. They could hear the ripple and flow of the Vistula, wind rustling the bushes along its bank. They turned to looked back. The glow of Auschwitz was visible, but the camp was silent from this distance. Knowing they needed to get off these open fields before sunrise, they risked standing up and walking quickly along the river.

The sky to the east lightened to a pale gray. Enough light to make out their next destination, a wall of trees a couple miles to the south. Enough light to read one of the signs they kept passing.

ATTENTION! FORBIDDEN ZONE! VIOLATORS SHOT WITHOUT WARNING!

They were still on land controlled by Auschwitz authorities, a sprawling territory cleared of Polish villages and farms. They wouldn't make it to the woods before daylight. Dropping back to the ground, they crawled toward the trees.

It took two hours to reach the woods. Under the cover of the boughs of fir trees, they allowed themselves a short rest.

The friends had talked over the plan many times in camp, never knowing if they'd make it this far. From here, they would turn east toward the Sola River, which flowed out of the mountains of Slovakia and provided an ideal north-south landmark. The Slovak border was about fifty miles to the south, a two- or three-day hike for someone traveling along roads in the open. This was obviously not an option. They'd have to wind their way around towns and farms, circle around lakes and marshes, sticking to patches of trees when possible, avoiding any human contact.

This was occupied territory, heavily patrolled by German soldiers and police. German settlers had forced Polish families out of their homes and were living on many of the farms Rudi and Fred would have to pass. Polish families still in the area might be willing to help—or they might turn Rudi and Fred over to authorities. Anyone caught helping an escaped prisoner knew they would be executed, along with their entire family.

Rudi and Fred would have to avoid even the smallest roads, moving only at night. First, they needed to get a little farther from Auschwitz. They got up and continued through the forest until they were stopped short by voices.

The voices of . . . *children*?

They dove into a clump of bushes. Through tangled branches they saw a few dozen boys with packs and matching uniforms of the Hitler Youth, a scouting organization designed to train young Nazis. Here were boys who'd know what to do if they spotted skinny guys with shaved heads hiding in the woods.

Just a hundred feet from Rudi and Fred's hiding spot, the boys took off their packs. They sat down and started eating lunch.

There was nothing to do but wait. An hour passed, or what felt like an hour. Then a bit of luck—it began to rain. The boys sat with their sandwiches, looking at one another but not moving, as if no one wanted to be the first to admit he was bothered by the chilly downpour. Finally, they got up and ran off.

Rudi and Fred rose from their puddle and hurried on, searching for a safer place to hide until dark. Their bare heads were soaked, but their feet in their fine boots were still dry.

They tightened their overcoats and kept moving south.

33

BY EARLY APRIL 1944, AMERICAN and British bombers had begun targeting German-occupied Hungary, smashing railways and factories. Soviet forces were fast approaching from the east.

Gerta and her mother had found what they'd hoped would be a safe spot, a small house on the edge of Budapest. Their goal was to stay in hiding long enough to find out where Max was imprisoned and get in touch with him. Help him, if possible.

There was no time.

The Nazis were moving quickly to round up Jews in the rural communities and small towns of Hungary. Police banged on the doors of Jewish homes and gave people a few minutes to pack a bag. Groups were forced to gather in local synagogues, then driven to ghettos in larger cities.

The SS told everyone that their labor was needed for "war production purposes."

Gerta and Jozefina feared their hiding place was no longer safe.

They decided their best chance would be to sneak back into their own country, Slovakia. Persecution of Jews had relaxed a bit there, they'd heard. Largely because there were so few left alive.

Two years before, Gerta and her mother had marched by night from Slovakia to Hungary. Back then they'd needed a guide. This time they traveled alone.

Filip Müller had never been so glad to live through a routine day in Auschwitz. The SS had wheeled out their mobile gallows—but had brought back no escaped prisoners to hang. The structures lurked in the courtyard as everyone went about their normal, horrible, daily tasks.

Filip felt more and more hopeful as the day went on. Rudi and Fred were out there somewhere. Getting farther away by the hour.

Of course, Filip knew his friends' corpses could be dragged back into camp at any moment. He knew how desperately the Nazis must be hunting them.

In fact, before Rudi and Fred even made it out of the lumber pile, camp officials had begun distributing a warrant for their arrest, notifying the Gestapo and other Nazi authorities throughout Poland and beyond. Every police station already knew the names of the escaped prisoners, their age and place of birth, and the numbers tattooed on their arms.

Rudi and Fred woke up at night and crawled out from under a tangle of bushes.

Wet and shivering, they rubbed their hands together, stamped their feet, scraped some of the mud off their clothes, and divided a chunk of bread. They ate as they marched through the dark woods, twigs snapping beneath their feet. They hurried up and down hills and splashed across shallow streams. Both took several falls, tripping on unseen tree roots.

The woods opened on a field. They moved quickly across the exposed space and were alarmed to see, ahead in the distance, the outline of watchtowers. The menacing outer cordon of another concentration camp. The towers, they knew, would be manned at dawn.

The map in Rudi's head was from a student's atlas printed before the war, before the Nazis built their camps in Poland. He and Fred had no way of knowing how to navigate around this obstacle. All they could do was pick a direction and keep moving.

Still dangerously near the camp, they spotted a stand of trees. It might be the best cover they were going to find before dawn. They ran for the trees and burrowed into what was already becoming a familiar spot—a tiny jungle of dense, wet bushes.

The sun rose. Birds chirped. It was a lovely April morning.

Except for one thing. They were in a public park.

When the friends peered out from their thicket, they saw uniformed SS men and their wives strolling along winding lanes. Children playing on the grass. Worst of all were the dogs. Happy dogs running free, chasing one another, exploring the glorious smells of spring.

Rudi and Fred spent an endless day in the bushes, hands on the handles of their knives. No chance for the sleep they so badly needed.

Never relax so long as you're in enemy territory.

Another of Dmitri's warnings. And that's what this was: enemy territory. Not a broad, dark forest, but farmland and villages, a mostly open and populated region of Nazi-occupied Poland.

In other words, never relax.

They crawled out of the bushes after dark. They shoved bent branches back into place, hoping to leave no clues behind. Rudi checked the knee he'd smashed on one of his falls. Bruised and swollen, it screamed every time he put weight on the leg.

But both of them were aching all over by now. They had to get moving.

They ate a small ration of bread as they walked. They stopped to drink from an icy stream. Exhausted and desperately hungry, weakened by two years of malnutrition and abuse, they struggled to climb hills. The friends pushed each other on, lifting each other up from falls, taking turns urging another hundred steps. Just another hundred. And now a hundred more. When they reached what looked like a good hiding spot, both dropped instantly into a deep sleep.

Night fell. They forced themselves to get up and move on. Damp and freezing, their hands and faces covered with mud and dried blood, they staggered through small forests and up and down steep slopes. As far as Rudi could tell, they were on course. They kept the Sola River to their left. To the right, they caught glimpses of a winding railway line approximately where it should be according to the map in Rudi's brain. But it was difficult to chart an accurate march in the dark. They knew they were off track when they saw the lights of a large town directly in their path.

The small city of Bielsko, Rudi figured. They'd drifted too far to the west.

They swung in an arc around town, but got turned around, and found themselves on paved streets. They raced forward in the shadows of stone buildings, guessing at turns, knowing they could run into a police patrol around any corner.

Knowing the Germans would be looking specifically for them.

By dawn they'd made it out of the maze, but were hopelessly far from cover, on a dirt road in some tiny village just outside the city. With their bony faces and muddy clothes, a week's growth on their shaved heads, they knew they had to get off the road right away.

There was no option now—they were going to have to seek help. They were going to have put their lives in the hands of a stranger.

How could they know which of these houses might belong to Germans who'd moved in since Hitler's takeover? How could they know which of the Polish families wouldn't immediately turn them over to the SS? They couldn't. They had to pick a house and hope.

They chose a humble-looking hut. Chickens pecked in the dirt yard. They walked around the side of the house and knocked on the back door.

34

THE DOOR OPENED. AN ELDERLY woman in a white scarf looked over the strangers.

"Praised be the name of Christ," Fred said, using a traditional Polish greeting.

"May His name be praised forever," the woman replied.

Fred's Polish was decent, but his accent exposed him as a foreigner. A teenage girl, visibly anxious, stepped up and stood behind the older woman. Both women looked from Fred to Rudi, at their stubbly scalps, their once-fine suits now torn and filthy. Both knew that helping men on the run could cost them their lives.

"Please come in, gentlemen," the old woman said.

She led them into a kitchen with a stone floor. She was calm, Rudi thought, not nervous. And there was something more in her expression. Something forceful. Defiant.

"I'm afraid my Russian is not very good, but you speak Polish well," she said. "You must be hungry."

So she thought they were Soviet soldiers, escaped prisoners of war. This proved the woman's courage—nothing would get her shot quicker than helping the Soviets.

The teenager set down bowls of potatoes. As Rudi and Fred shoveled food into their mouths, the old woman warned them that the Germans had taken over villages all around. Settlers were well armed and trained to shoot strangers on sight. German police and soldiers patrolled the region, hunting for partisan rebels.

"If my sons were here, they might be able to give you more help," she told them. "But one is dead, and the other is in some concentration camp."

What can you say to a mother about that?

Rudi and Fred chopped a pile of wood for the women. They ate another meal and fell asleep inside. The old woman shook them awake in the middle of the night. As they pulled on their coats to leave, she held a few coins out to Rudi.

He hesitated, thinking of Dmitri's advice against carrying money. Also, it was obvious this woman was very poor, and she'd done so much for them already.

"Please take it," she said. "Just for luck."

Rudi put the coins in his pocket. He and Fred thanked the woman and continued their journey.

Rudi and Fred approached Slovakia from the north. Gerta and her mother neared the border from the south.

Gerta and Jozefina—two rural Hungarian women, as far as anyone could tell—took a train to a town near the frontier. They hid in the woods until dark, watching passing patrols, timing their patterns.

In the middle of the night, they crossed into their country. Risking an early morning bus, they reached the capital city, Bratislava.

Gerta decided her parents had protected her long enough. Now, at seventeen, *she* took the lead.

She'd heard that a friend, Josef Weiss, one of the boys who used to come to their conversations in the meadow, was still in Slovakia. He'd been deemed an "economically useful Jew" by the government, and thus allowed to stay and work in Bratislava. Gerta arranged a meeting at Josef's apartment, and she and her mother rode a tram to the outskirts of town.

Josef hugged Gerta, astonished to see her alive. His whole family had been deported in 1942. There'd been no word from anyone.

"I guess I know what you need from me," he said. "You will have to have forged papers."

He was right, of course. Gerta and her mother had to become Christian Slovaks.

"Actually, you're in luck," Josef told them. A friend of his had managed to steal a stack of blank identity cards from a government office in eastern Slovakia. The village was now in the hands of the Soviet Union's Red Army, which meant the Slovak government couldn't check its own records from that part of the country.

Gerta and Jozefina picked a new last name, but decided to keep their real first names and birthdays—two less things to remember. As they were getting ready to leave, Josef pulled Gerta aside. He told her that he was part of a small underground resistance network.

"No one would guess that you are Jewish, with your blond hair and blue eyes," he said. "Would you like to work with our organization?"

It would have been much safer for Gerta to say no, to lay low until the end of the war.

Instead, she jumped at the chance.

Rudi and Fred zigzagged between patches of forest for two more nights, making cautious and painfully slow progress toward Slovakia. The mountains rose higher as they moved south, with patches of snow in shady spots. Their supply of bread was gone.

The next landmark was Porąbka, halfway to the border. The place where Sandor Eisenbach and his friends had been captured.

Steer clear of that place. It's stinking with soldiers.

And there it was, deep in a valley, like an image on a postcard. A town beside a blue lake created by a dam on the Sola River.

Rudi looked down at the buildings, touching the coins in his pocket. It would be so easy. Slip into town, find a little store. An hour from now they could be back in the mountains, wolfing down bread and cheese.

His belly was roaring for food. He was so tempted to risk it. He would have, if not for Dmitri's voice in his head.

They moved on, past Porąbka, sticking to the wooded mountains west of the Sola.

No rest at night. That was the plan. But their bodies were breaking down. Later that night, they stopped on a dark hill, spread their overcoats on the damp grass, and collapsed.

Rudi's eyes were closed when he heard the first shot.

The bullet tore over his head and thumped into the earth. Rudi and Fred leapt to their feet and ran, leaving their coats behind, stumbling up the exposed slope.

German soldiers, ten or twelve of them, opened fire from another hilltop, about a hundred yards away. Fred dove behind a boulder. Rudi, a few steps behind, tripped and went down face-first. Bullets pierced the dirt all around him, pinged off rocks. Rudi lay still, too scared to move.

"We've got him!" one of the Germans shouted.

The soldiers charged down the hill toward their prey.

"Head for the trees!" Fred called.

Fred and Rudi scrambled up and over the top of their hill. They barreled down the other side and straight into a stream running deep and fast with snowmelt. The icy current knocked Rudi over. He went under completely, fought to get his head to the surface, and went under again, twisting and tumbling, clawing his way to the far bank.

They both made it across and lay for a moment in the slushy mud, shivering and panting. Heaving themselves up, they climbed the bank and raced for a pine forest halfway up the next slope.

The stream saved them. The soldiers didn't cross the swollen stream.

Rudi and Fred reached the trees and kept going, kept running until they heard no more soldiers' shouts, no more gunshots. Long past the point of exhaustion, the friends somehow found the strength to quicken their pace as they moved into the more rugged terrain near the border.

They stopped to hide when the sun rose. Rudi's feet were so swollen that he could no longer get his boots off. Fred pulled his off and wrapped his blistered feet in bloodstained rags. Both shivered without their coats. Too unnerved to sleep, they pushed on by daylight, sticking to remote mountain paths.

Nine days after crawling under the wires of Auschwitz, Rudi and Fred were hurrying across an overgrown meadow above the town of Milówka when they practically collided with a Polish woman.

35

SHE WAS AN ELDERLY WOMAN, a local farmer, judging by her simple dress. She stared at the young men, showing no reaction Rudi could read.

But he and Fred had just emerged from the woods covered with dirt and dried blood, their ragged suits sour with sweat. She would recognize men on the run. She would know the Germans would kill her for offering help.

There was no point in lying, Rudi decided.

"We're heading for the Slovak border," he said in his best Polish. "Can you show us the way? We've escaped from a concentration camp, from Auschwitz."

He hadn't planned on saying that last part; it just came out. But he was glad he'd done it. Now, no matter what, at least one person would know their story.

The woman turned and looked toward the taller peaks to the southeast, the direction they'd need to travel. Turning back to Rudi and Fred she said, "Wait here. Tonight, I'll send a man who will help you. And I'll send you some food."

She walked downhill across the meadow, crossed a footbridge over a stream, and disappeared from view.

Rudi and Fred had to make a quick decision. Should they wait? They desperately needed to eat—but could this woman be trusted? Was she already on her way to alert the Germans?

The footbridge was maybe half a mile away. In the other direction, about two hundred yards from where they stood, was a forest. If they saw German soldiers coming over the bridge, they might have time to run for the trees. It was worth the risk, they agreed. They wouldn't make it much farther without food.

Two hours later, someone appeared on the bridge. A small boy. He walked uphill toward Rudi and Fred, holding something wrapped in a cloth.

They let the child approach. He held out the cloth. They unwrapped the package and gazed at the stunning vision: boiled potatoes and a chunk of meat.

The boy smiled and said, "My grandmother will be back when it is dark."

The temperature fell as the sun set. Rudi and Fred huddled, teeth chattering. They couldn't see the bridge in the faint moonlight, but hoped they'd at least hear the clomp of boots on the planks if soldiers came their way.

They were famished again but had at least eaten something. Was it best to move on? Risk the rugged mountains without a guide?

Too late. Two figures were already crossing the meadow. They'd never heard footsteps on the bridge.

It was the grandmother, holding a parcel, and a man about her age, a Polish farmer, with a pistol in his hand. Rudi and Fred reached for the handles of their knives.

The woman walked up, with no fear of the strangers. "Here's some more food," she said.

They let go of their knives and ate like ravenous dogs.

The man with the gun watched in silence, then slid the pistol into his jacket and let out an enormous laugh. "You're from a concentration camp, all right," he said. "Only really hungry men could eat like that."

He'd been wary of a trap. The Germans knew that people in town sometimes helped anti-Nazi partisans—maybe they'd dressed two agents as runaway prisoners to entrap the locals. He'd heard of Rudi and Fred. Everyone had. They'd all seen the warrant for two Slovak Jews from Auschwitz, and they were expected to help apprehend the fugitives.

"You'd better come with me," the man told them. "You can stay the night in my place, and tomorrow night I'll see you safely across the border."

Rudi's feet were so swollen and tender, he could barely walk. Fred helped him totter through fields to a small cottage in a valley. Rudi fell into a chair, pulled out his knife, and cut the boots off his feet.

The friends slept through the rest of the night and into the following day.

When the man returned from work in the early evening, he

briefed them on what to expect in the mountains. The border was patrolled, but the guards stuck to a routine, which should give them a chance to slip through. "Do exactly what I say," he said. "I'll get you across."

He handed Rudi a pair of carpet slippers, the only footwear he could spare, and said, "It's time to go."

They hiked out of the valley. Rudi was amazed at how quickly the old man slid through the dark forest, how little sound he made. On aching feet in house slippers, he struggled to keep up. The man stopped suddenly. Rudi wasn't sure why. This spot looked like any other in the woods.

"A German patrol passes here every ten minutes," the man whispered, checking his watch. "We'll have to let the next one go by."

All three of them ducked into the bushes. They heard boots on dirt, snapping twigs. German soldiers marched past, close enough to touch.

Without their guide, Rudi and Fred would have walked right into the patrol.

A few minutes later they were on the move again. They followed the man all night, up and down slopes, along narrow paths they'd never have found, past German patrols they never could have avoided on their own.

Early in the morning, before dawn, their guide led them to the edge of the woods. He pointed to a sloping meadow. Just visible across the open field was the black wall of another stand of trees.

"See that forest over there?" the man said. "That's Slovakia."

Their country was fifty yards away. Rudi and Fred tensed for a dash to the border.

The Germans patrolled this clearing, the old man warned. "You'd better wait until the next bunch appears before you move on."

Rudi and Fred never asked their guide his name. If they were caught and tortured, it would be better not to know. But they whispered their thanks.

"Glad I could help," the man said. Looking down at Rudi's feet and grinning, he added, "I hope the slippers hold out!"

And he was gone.

One last time, Rudi and Fred crouched in the bushes.

A German patrol marched across the meadow.

The two friends forced themselves to wait a few more minutes. Then they got up and ran.

A little over two years since getting into a taxi outside his home, in the tattered remains of a suit taken from a dead prisoner, wearing a belt from a dead friend and slippers from a Polish farmer whose name he'd never know, Rudi Vrba crossed the border into Slovakia.

36

THEY'D COME SO FAR, DODGED so many dangers. But the job was far from done.

Slovakia was still led by Jozef Tiso, still patrolled by Hlinka guards. For a couple of Jewish fugitives, by far the safest move would be to stay in the mountains, link up with a partisan group fighting the pro-Hitler government. And they planned to do this.

But not yet.

After a two-hour hike through the forest, they came to a small farm. A man was working the field with his horse. The farmer stopped his work and stared as two strangers came out of the trees. Filthy men in rags, all scratched up. Partisans? Smugglers? They'd been living rough, that's for sure.

Dmitri had told Rudi to trust no one. Good advice, but they'd never have made it this far without help.

"Where are we?" Rudi asked, finally switching back to his native language.

"Near the village of Skalité," the man told them.

Rudi could picture the location. Čadca, a larger town, was ten or fifteen miles away.

"We must get to Čadca," Rudi said.

The farmer smiled. "You're not going to get far in those clothes."

The man led them to his cottage. According to a calendar on the wall it was April 21. Two weeks since they'd jumped into the lumber pile in Auschwitz.

The farmer introduced himself as Andrej Čánecký. He gave them food and clean, well-worn work clothes. They told him a short version of their story, explaining that they needed to get in contact with leaders of the Jewish community in Slovakia, if there were any still around.

Čánecký said he knew of a Jewish doctor in Čadca, a Dr. Pollack. Tiso had exempted some Jewish doctors from resettlement, putting them to work in small towns to show his "love" of the rural population.

Rudi actually remembered a Dr. Pollack—he'd met him in the Nováky transport camp, way back in June 1942. Could be the same man, Rudi figured. They'd go and see him right away.

Not so fast, Čánecký cautioned. They couldn't just stroll down the road without papers, without a good reason to be hiking across the countryside. He was going to Čadca himself in three days, bringing some pigs to the weekend market. They could come along, playing the role of his farmhands.

Rudi and Fred spent three days in the farmer's cottage, mostly eating and sleeping.

In Bratislava, Gerta's friend Josef introduced her to members of the Jewish underground, young men and women who forged documents and distributed them to people in hiding. They desperately needed access to typewriters, which were nearly impossible to find during wartime.

Years before, after being kicked out of school, Gerta had made a half-hearted attempt to learn secretarial skills. Her typing was rusty at this point, her shorthand nearly nonexistent. Undaunted, with her forged identity papers in hand, Gerta walked into a large office building and applied for work as a secretary.

A woman gave her a typing test. Gerta did well enough to move on to a shorthand exam. The woman dictated a two-page letter. When it was time to type up her notes, Gerta couldn't read her own scribbles. Relying on her strong memory, she re-created the letter with impressive accuracy.

She got the job, assigned to be the personal secretary of a friendly young man named Martin. She asked Martin if she could stay late some evenings to type her personal letters. He thought that sounded fine.

Josef provided Gerta with blank identity cards and birth certificate forms, and Gerta took the enormous risk of using her office typewriter to forge new papers for refugees.

"I was thrilled," she'd later say. "At last I was part of a group of people that worked hard to save lives."

When Saturday arrived, Rudi and Fred walked with Andrej Čánecký to the Čadca market, driving ten pigs along with them. It was a dizzying sensation to travel openly along a country road under the warm spring sun.

Čánecký sold his pigs, then showed his guests to the building where Dr. Pollack had his office. He wished them luck and walked off. Rudi and Fred turned to look at the large building. Armed soldiers stood guard at the front door.

It was the local headquarters of the Slovak army.

Just in case they'd forgotten that everything they'd done could come crashing down at any moment. Just in case they'd forgotten that all it would take would be one slipup, one bad break, and they'd be on the train back to Auschwitz. Not as slave laborers this time. As dead men walking.

"To hell with it," Fred said. "Can't we be sick, just like anybody else?"

Rudi agreed. They looked reasonably like a couple of young farmhands, or maybe new army recruits. Anyway, they'd come too far to be scared off now.

They walked through the front door. The guards never even turned their heads.

They found the doctor's office and waited their turn. Rudi was called in first. He recognized Pollack, but the man clearly didn't know him. How could he? Rudi had changed a lot over the last two years.

Dr. Pollack asked what the trouble was.

"I'm a bit shy ... ," Rudi began, hesitating. "There's a nurse ..."

The doctor nodded. So it was *that* sort of trouble. He asked the nurse to step out of the examination room.

"I've not much time," Dr. Pollack said as the door closed. "Pull down the trousers."

No, Rudi said, there was nothing wrong in the trousers. He'd just wanted to be alone with the doctor. He reminded Pollack that they'd met before and, very briefly, told his story.

The doctor was astonished. No Jew had ever come back from "resettlement."

How could anyone get out of Auschwitz? How could they cross occupied Poland? He'd heard that prisoners were tattooed and asked, with apologies, to see Rudi's arm.

Rudi pushed up his sleeve to reveal the numbers: 44070.

The doctor went pale. He'd been permitted to keep his wife and children with him. But his parents, his brothers and sisters, and their families—they had all been sent away.

They were almost certainly dead, Rudi told the doctor.

Until that moment, Pollack had allowed himself to hope his relatives were in some sort of resettlement area, suffering perhaps, but hanging on. Visibly shaken, he wrapped bandages around Rudi's blistered feet—he had to do *something* to justify the visit, and Rudi's feet really were in awful shape.

"Tonight, you sleep at my place," Dr. Pollack told Rudi. "Tomorrow, I'll take you to the leaders of the Jewish community in Žilina."

GREATER
GERMANY

Oświęcim

× Auschwitz–Birkenau

Jawischowitz

River Vistula

Kęty

Pisarzowice

Bielsko-Biała

Kozy

Porąbka

POLAND

Krobacza Laka Mountain

River Sola

Żywiec

PROTECTORATE OF
BOHEMIA AND
MORAVIA

Milówka

Zwardoń

Rajcza

Skalité

Sól

Čadca

Beskid Mountains

Žilina

SLOVAKIA

ESCAPE ROUTE, 1944

⟶ Escape Route

⫘⫘⫘⫘ Railway

--- International Borders

15 kilometers

10 miles

37

THE NEXT HURDLE WAS GETTING people to believe them.

The friends traveled by train to Žilina to meet with Jewish leaders left in the city. About two-thirds of Slovakia's Jewish population was gone, having been deported in 1942. Fewer than twenty-five thousand Jewish citizens remained, either in labor camps or in the country with government permission because they did work that was considered vital to the economy.

Members of the local Jewish council welcomed Rudi and Fred to their office. The men had heard rumors of horrific conditions at Auschwitz, but never a firsthand report of the mass murder taking place there. Like Dr. Pollack, they'd clung to the hope that the people who'd been "resettled" might still be alive. They asked Rudi and Fred to make separate statements, so that neither's testimony would influence the other's.

Rudi sat in a bare basement room with members of the council. He drew sketches of the camp from memory. He dictated for six hours, pouring out the volumes of information in his head, everything he'd seen in the Canada Command warehouses and on the train platform, all the people he'd seen driven in trucks to the crematoria, everything Filip Müller had witnessed in those buildings. He described the new rail line leading right to the gas chambers, and the urgent need to warn the world about what Hitler had planned for the Jews of Hungary.

Down the hall, in another room, Fred Wetzler was doing the exact same thing.

These were the first detailed, eyewitness accounts of the Auschwitz death factory to reach the outside world.

The Jewish leaders promised to write up a report and distribute it to contacts across Europe and beyond. Rudi slumped in his chair, the terrible burden finally off his back.

"Relief suddenly struck me with all the force of a physical blow," he'd say of this moment. "I had done what I had set out to do."

What impact would their report have? How many lives would be saved? Rudi and Fred had no idea. But they *did* know they were still fugitives from the Nazis. With new clothes, cash, and false identity papers provided by Jewish leaders in Žilina, the friends traveled to a small town in the Tatra Mountains in eastern Slovakia and tried to settle into the tranquil routine of ordinary students enjoying a summer holiday.

"O.K. We'll go."

With these words on June 5, 1944, U.S. General Dwight Eisenhower launched the largest amphibious invasion in history. More than 150,000 troops from the United States, Britain, Canada, and other Allied nations crossed the English Channel toward the north-western coast of Nazi-occupied France. Early the next morning—D-Day—the soldiers stormed the heavily fortified coastline and fought their way up the beaches.

This was another major turning point of World War II. Finally, after years of bloody fighting against Axis forces in North Africa and Italy, the Allies cracked open the western edge of Hitler's European fortress.

Allied soldiers liberated Paris in August and continued fighting their way toward Germany. At the same time, in the east, the massive Red Army was rolling straight for the German capital of Berlin.

Even now, as their empire crumbled, the Nazis directed their dwindling resources to mass murder, racing to deport the Jewish population of Hungary to Auschwitz. There was no way these transports could be kept secret from the people of Slovakia—the long, crowded trains had to cross Slovakia on their way north to occupied Poland.

Rudi heard about the trains. He knew where they were headed. He knew exactly where the journey would end.

"Why did I escape?" he roared in frustration and fury. "What was the point?"

Rudi had no way to know that the eyewitness report he and Fred Wetzler had brought out of Auschwitz was moving. The report was moving slowly—too slowly—but it *was* moving.

The document that would go down in history as the Vrba-Wetzler Report reached Switzerland in the middle of June 1944. The BBC broadcast passages of the report on the radio, and articles based on the escaped prisoners' stunning testimony began appearing in British and American newspapers. The *New York Times* printed details about Nazi atrocities at Auschwitz that had clearly come from Filip Müller: "Prisoners were led into cells and ordered to strip for bathing. Then cyanide gas was said to have been released, causing death in three to five minutes."

U.S. President Franklin Roosevelt appealed directly to the Hungarian ruler, Miklós Horthy, to stop the deportation of Hungarian Jews. Similar demands came from the British government, King Gustav of Sweden, the International Committee of the Red Cross, and Pope Pius XII in Rome.

On July 2, U.S. bombers hit oil refineries and rail yards in Budapest. Horthy assumed there must be a connection between the bombing and Roosevelt's threats. In fact, the attack was part of a wider Allied campaign to take out Axis energy and transportation assets.

Still, Horthy was feeling the heat. He'd joined up with Hitler when the Germans were winning. Now Hitler looked doomed, and Horthy decided that at this point he had more to fear from the Allies.

On July 7, Horthy gave the order to halt the deportation of Jews from Hungary.

The Nazis did not have sufficient forces in Hungary to continue their operations without Hungarian compliance.

Still, there are no storybook endings here.

More than four hundred thousand Hungarian Jews had already been deported to Auschwitz. A small percentage had been selected for forced labor. The vast majority of these men, women, and children were murdered in the gas chambers.

But more than two hundred thousand Jews were still in Hungary, mainly in Budapest. Thanks in large part to the escape and testimony of Rudolf Vrba and Alfred Wetzler, two hundred thousand people who had been slated for Auschwitz were still alive.

British historian Martin Gilbert later concluded: "No other single act in the Second World War saved so many Jews from the fate that Hitler and the SS had determined for them."

38

RUDI AND FRED WOULD NOT know the full impact of their heroic actions until much later.

Posing as vacationing students in eastern Slovakia, they drank beer in cafés, flirted with local women, hiked in the green mountains. It was no good. They could never really enjoy the experiences. They couldn't simply set aside two years of relentless terror, two years of unbroken focus on surviving one moment to the next. Rudi felt himself tense up every time he saw a man in uniform. Whenever a Hlinka guard asked to see his papers, he coiled his strength and anger for a fight to the death.

When Rudi's thick black hair grew in, he went to a barber for a trim—and nearly bumped into an SS officer in the doorway.

The man clicked his heels and smiled. "After you, sir."

Rudi gave a small nod of thanks. He sat in one of the barber's chairs. The Nazi sat beside him. As the barbers worked, the Nazi offered Rudi a cigarette, even lit it for him, and attempted a few friendly phrases of Slovak.

The entire time Rudi was thinking: *What would this man do if he knew who I was? How differently would this seemingly nice, normal man behave inside the wires of Auschwitz?*

"There were times when we wondered whether we would ever be happy again," Rudi would later write of his feelings that summer. "These were somber moments in which we feared that never again, perhaps, would we be able to live normal lives."

Annoyed by his pleasant life in the mountains, restless to find some way to take more direct action, Rudi slipped into Bratislava.

One day that summer, when Gerta met Josef to hand over a new batch of forged documents, Josef told her that he'd just seen one of their friends from Trnava: Rudi Vrba.

"Would you like to see him?" Josef asked.

Gerta was stunned, overwhelmed with joy. Rudi was alive! The clever boy she'd fallen for as a girl, what seemed like a lifetime ago. Yes, of course she wanted to see him!

"He has changed a lot," Josef cautioned. "He's not the same innocent child you remember."

"Well, isn't that true of all of us?" Gerta asked. "We've all changed."

That was true. Every Jewish person in Europe who'd survived this far into World War II had a story to tell.

Of course, Gerta had no idea how horrible Rudi's story would be.

Josef said he'd arrange for all three of them to meet the following afternoon in a park by the Danube. Gerta stayed up all night picturing a movie-like reunion with Rudi, a passionate kiss by the river. Unable to focus at work the next day, she told her boss she had a headache, and he let her leave early. She walked to the Danube and sat on the grass, listening to the water, watching the pebbly beach sparkle in the sun.

She jumped up when she saw Rudi coming—then froze when she saw his face.

Was this the boy I remembered and had loved just two years ago? she wondered. *Could any person change that much in only two years?*

It was his eyes. His eyes had always twinkled with intelligence and mischievous wit. Now Gerta saw reservation. Sadness.

The three friends sat by the river. Rudi had just begun to tell his story when Josef cut in, changing the subject to pleasant small talk.

Rudi and Gerta agreed to meet alone the next afternoon for a swim.

Again, Gerta was early. She found a shady spot beneath a willow tree and sat on a towel.

Rudi walked down the path. He was smiling, but not with his eyes. When she hugged him, she felt his body tense. She suggested a swim—something normal, carefree, like the old days.

He took off his shirt. Her eyes locked on the tattoo on his arm.

"What are you staring at?" he snapped, his face twisting into a bitter grin, an expression of pain and hatred. "This is my identity. For two years I had no name, I was just 44070. Where do you think I spent those two years?"

They sat down together. Neither spoke for a while. Rudi put his arm around Gerta's shoulder. She leaned her head on his chest. Rudi apologized. She'd understand better, he said, when she heard his story.

He talked for an hour. He told her what he'd seen at Auschwitz.

Gerta could not understand how the sky stayed blue. How did the river keep running, the stones keep sparkling? How could such normal things, such beautiful things, exist alongside the scenes Rudi was describing?

"Neither of us could think of swimming, or even staying in this peaceful place," Gerta later said. "We dressed and returned to the dusty city. We walked quietly, holding hands."

In late July 1944, the Red Army entered Lublin, Poland, and liberated the Majdanek concentration camp.

When Rudi had been held there in the spring of 1942, Majdanek had not yet been a killing center. Later that year, however, the SS had added gas chambers. By the summer of 1944, Hitler's forces were in such rapid retreat they did not have time to destroy the evidence.

Now, for the first time, photographers and film crews from Allied countries recorded images of a Nazi death camp. Reporters began collecting the testimony of surviving prisoners. The staggering, heartbreaking process of amassing the story of the Holocaust had begun.

"I have just seen the most terrible place on the face of the earth," the journalist W. H. Lawrence wrote in the *New York Times* in August. Lawrence described a gas chamber disguised as a shower building, five furnaces used to burn bodies, and mass graves of bodies the Nazis did not have time to burn.

"I have talked with German officers attached to the camp," Lawrence reported, "who admitted quite frankly that it was a highly systemized place for annihilation."

In September 1944, Rudolf Vrba turned twenty.

The Allied advance continued, closing in on Germany from east and west. Adolf Hitler lived in underground bunkers, stooped over and visibly aged, throwing feeble tantrums at the parade of disastrous news.

In Slovakia, partisan fighters rose in open rebellion against the pro-Nazi government. Thousands of German troops poured into Slovakia to smash the uprising. Rudi volunteered to join the Slovak partisans and, after some very brief training, was thrown into combat.

On a night in October, with a submachine gun over his shoulder, Rudi marched with about 120 rebels into the small town of Stará Turá in the mountains of western Slovakia, slipping through dark streets toward a schoolhouse that hundreds of German soldiers had made their local base.

Rudi's commander gave the signal. The men opened fire and charged.

Return gunfire burst from the doors and windows of the school. Men around Rudi were screaming, blasting away, hurling grenades. Rudi felt tears streaming down his face. In the chaos and violence of his first firefight, he was so happy, he was crying.

He was not running away anymore. He was running forward.

39

A MONTH LATER THE NAZIS came for Gerta.

They struck in the middle of the night, pounding on the door of Gerta and her mother's Bratislava apartment.

"Open up! This is the Gestapo!"

When the women opened the door in their robes, two Gestapo agents ordered them to get dressed. Gerta threw on clothes, dropping two apples into her coat pocket as she walked toward the front door. Was there any chance for escape? No, she saw—the Nazi police blocked the only way out to the street.

"Move faster," they ordered. "We haven't got all night just for you."

Even as Hitler's armies collapsed, the Nazis were racing to round up remaining Jews in Slovakia. Gerta had hoped their false identity papers would keep them hidden—but something had gone wrong. Someone must have recognized her or Jozefina, followed them home, informed on them.

The agents shoved Gerta and Jozefina into the back of a car and drove them to the local Gestapo headquarters. Separated from her mother, Gerta was thrown into a chair in a tiny room, a bright bulb aimed into her eyes.

As her eyes adjusted to the light, Gerta got a look at her interrogator. A pale, cruel-looking officer of about forty. He roared at her in German, cursing her as a "filthy Jew."

She fought to hide her terror. Her one chance, she sensed, was to act like an innocent teen. She reached into her pocket and pulled out an apple. She forced herself to smile like a kid.

"Would you like an apple?"

The man stopped, stunned. He'd been about to start beating this girl, and she offers him a snack?

She saw it on his face: a split second of doubt. Was it possible they'd arrested the wrong person? The apple trick saved Gerta.

Warning, "We'll talk again tomorrow," the man tossed her into a dark cell.

About thirty people lay on the bare, freezing floor. Gerta found Jozefina huddled in a corner, using her coat as a blanket. Her lips were blue, her face bruised and swollen. She attempted a smile when she saw her daughter. One of her teeth had been knocked out.

"I didn't tell them anything," Jozefina said. "And you, Gerti, are you all right?"

Gerta put her arm around her mother. "I'm fine," she said. "We must get out of here, that is all that matters now, to get out of here together."

Gerta had not told her mother the stories she'd heard from Rudi. She'd meant to, but now was not the time. Her mother was already so frightened.

* * *

From inside the Gestapo building, prisoners could hear the sounds of air-raid sirens and explosions in the city. Allied planes were bombing an oil refinery in Bratislava—and Gerta secretly cheered them on.

The end of the war was so close.

Gestapo agents questioned Gerta and Jozefina for three days straight, accusing them of hiding their Jewish identity. The police starved and beat both women, but were rougher with Jozefina. At night she came back to the cell bloodied, beyond exhausted. She'd always been the rock of the family, the quickest to adapt to new situations. Now, for the first time, she looked fragile.

"Mum, listen to me," Gerta told her on their third night in prison. "We will get out of here, I promise, and we will survive, but please do not give up."

The interrogations continued. Gestapo agents searched Gerta and Jozefina's apartment—and found a stack of blank birth certificate forms Gerta had hidden. The police beat both women again. On their fifth day in custody, Jozefina confessed to her true identity.

Their time was up, Gerta knew. Soon they'd be on a train to Auschwitz. That night, on the cold floor of their cell, Gerta told her mother the stories she'd heard from Rudi. They must *not* get on that train. The last two days, between interrogations, the police had put both women to work cleaning the Gestapo offices above the prison cells. This, Gerta suggested, might give them a chance to get away.

"Forgive me, Gerti," Jozefina said, tears running down her cheeks. "If you can escape and fight on your own, please do so, but I can't follow you. I have neither the strength, nor the will to live after what you have told me."

Gerta held her mother. She idolized and loved this woman, and could not imagine life without her. "Still, I wasn't sure of my feelings," she'd later explain. "My wish to live was stronger than anything else."

Their sixth day in custody was cold, with heavy rain. Before sunrise, the police hauled Gerta and Jozefina up to the second floor, ordering them to clean offices overlooking the building's front entrance. When she opened the large windows to shake out her duster, Gerta noticed there were no guards posted at the front gate—maybe, she figured, because of the rain.

This was their chance, Gerta whispered to her mother. They needed to jump out the window. *Right now.*

Jozefina hesitated. She did not have the energy to go back on the run.

Gerta faced an impossible choice, with no time to think. She could stay with her mother, or she could fight to survive. For the rest of her long life, Gerta would wonder if she'd done the right thing.

She jumped out of the window.

She landed hard on the pavement and sprinted into the street. What now?

Her blouse and skirt were immediately soaked by the pounding rain. There was no way she'd go unnoticed for long. She had no friends who weren't in hiding, nothing but a few small coins in her shirt pocket.

She pictured Rudi, fighting in the mountains. She wished she could join him—but how?

Was there anyone she could turn to for help? What about her

nice-seeming boss, Martin? She had no idea if she could trust the man but could think of no better plan. Ducking into a phone box, she dialed the office number. Martin picked up.

Gerta told him she was in trouble. She asked to meet him. Martin suggested a coffeehouse near the office.

Had he called the Gestapo as soon as he'd hung up with her? That would be the smart thing to do, the best way to protect himself and his family.

Gerta hurried to the coffeehouse. She hid in a doorway across the street, watching. Martin walked in. He was alone. Gerta waited to see if he had been followed. Then she entered.

Her boss was sitting at a little table. Gerta joined him, her hair and clothes dripping. The strangest thing was that Martin did not seem surprised by any of this.

He must have known her secret all along, she figured.

Martin ordered hot coffee and cakes. He waited for Gerta to speak. She told him everything—that she was Jewish and had deceived him to get her job, that her parents were both in Nazi custody, that she'd just escaped from the Gestapo. Her only hope, she explained, was to get out of the country, get back to Hungary, but she'd need money and new papers, and a place to hide while arranging travel.

Gerta was putting Martin in terrible danger. She watched him think for a long moment. The silence at the table seemed endless.

"Yes," Martin finally said. "I will help you."

40

IN LATE NOVEMBER 1944, GERTA made her third midnight border crossing of the war. She arrived in Budapest on her eighteenth birthday, once again a refugee without identity papers.

That same week, Heinrich Himmler ordered the gas chambers at Auschwitz destroyed.

Soviet forces were closing in. The Nazis were running out of time, and the SS leader was desperate to hide as much of the evidence of mass murder as possible. Filip Müller was among the prisoners put to work dumping the ash of human remains into the Vistula River. He watched the SS burn camp records, set fire to the Canada warehouses, and dynamite the crematorium buildings.

On January 17, 1945, with Soviet artillery pounding in the distance, the Nazis evacuated Auschwitz. Filip was among more than fifty thousand prisoners forced to march west in the falling snow. When the first Soviet soldiers entered camp, they found ruined buildings, and about seventy-five hundred prisoners—the ones who were too weak to walk away.

After marching for days, Filip and the other prisoners were forced onto trains. They huddled in open boxcars without food. Many died of hunger and cold. The train crossed the border into northern Austria, dumping them at yet another concentration camp, Mauthausen.

Still an enslaved laborer, Filip was put to work in an aircraft factory. He held on, barely, until April. When Allied bombers began hitting nearby targets, SS guards marched the prisoners into a small camp in the forest, shooting anyone who fell behind.

Then the Nazis disappeared. Ran for their lives.

By this point, Filip was near death from starvation. He lay in a bunk, too weak to move, drifting in and out of consciousness. And then:

"We are free!"

"We are free!"

Filip had dreamt of this moment for three years. Now it was here, and he was too weak to feel anything. He dropped out of his bunk, crawled out the door, and passed out.

He woke to the roar of engines. Staggering through the woods to a small road, he looked out at a long, rumbling line of American tanks.

It was over. He'd made it.

Filip Müller was twenty-three. He would live to be ninety-one. He would live, and he would tell his story.

Soviet troops battled their way into the German capital of Berlin. On April 30, 1945, Adolf Hitler died by suicide in his underground bunker. On May 8, Germany surrendered to the Allies. The war in Europe was over.

Heinrich Himmler shaved off his Hitler mustache, covered one eye with a black patch, and tried to slip through an Allied checkpoint. Alert British soldiers grabbed him and dragged him to a prisoner of war camp. Before he could be questioned, Himmler bit down on a cyanide capsule he'd hidden in his mouth. He died writhing on the floor.

Gerta survived the last months of the war in Hungary. Even after all her close calls, she chose not to play it safe. As soon as she got back to Budapest, Gerta joined the Jewish underground and helped distribute forged identity papers to people in hiding.

When the fighting ended, she began to search for her parents. As survivors returned from concentration camps, they reported to Jewish community centers and posted their names and addresses on the walls. Gerta read through the lists day after day. There was nothing about Max or Jozefina.

Gerta wrote her own name—her real name—and pinned it to the wall. She then traveled back to Slovakia to continue the search in her hometown.

"Everything was the same," she'd say of Trnava, "and yet different from what I remembered." The buildings hadn't changed. But so many of the people were gone.

She walked to her old house, the home she'd left so suddenly more than three years before. She stepped up to the front door and rang the bell.

Mr. Šimončič—the man who'd taken over her family's shop, the father of Marushka, who'd once been her good friend—opened the door. Gerta saw horror flash across the man's face.

"Oh God," he said, "you are still alive."

Gerta asked if she could have a room in the house. She had nowhere to stay.

"We have nowhere else to go and we need the whole house," the man grumbled. "You can't just turn up and expect us to move out."

Soviet soldiers, who now occupied the town, forced Mr. Šimončič to let Gerta use one room of the house. Day after day, she read through updated lists of survivors posted on the walls of the Red Cross office and the Jewish community center. She never found a trace of her mother or father.

As her hope faded, Gerta walked the streets of her hometown. She stood outside the gate of her old school, the same gate that had locked her out nearly six years before. Students streamed outside, some her own age, some she recognized.

They did not seem to notice she was there.

Six weeks after arriving, Gerta decided to move on. Soviet authorities helped her regain legal ownership of her family home, but she didn't want to stay, and offered the building to a neighbor who'd always been kind to her. He wanted it, but had no money. Gerta agreed to give him the house in exchange for a camera, a type-writer, a gold watch—and one condition: the Šimončič family must be immediately evicted.

Rudi Vrba served with the Slovak freedom fighters through the end of the war. The newly reestablished government of Czechoslovakia awarded him its highest medal for valor in combat.

In May 1945, Rudi returned to Bratislava and was amazed to find that his mother had survived the war. Shipped to the Theresien-stadt concentration camp, she had persuaded guards to let her set up a little clothing workshop, promising to sew garments for their wives and girlfriends. She saved the lives of several prisoners by teaching them to make clothes.

Rudi reconnected with Gerta, who was back from her trip to Trnava. They had their whole lives ahead of them.

What should they do next?

The obvious answer was college—but neither had finished high school. When they heard the government was offering courses for young people who'd missed school during the war, Rudi and Gerta rushed to sign up. Cramming years of learning into three months, they attended classes every day for ten hours, then studied through the night, Rudi in his mother's apartment, Gerta in a room she shared with a friend. "We hardly slept at all," Gerta recalled, "but our desire to pass the exams at the end of the three months so that we could start university in September was so strong that it suppressed our need for sleep."

After the tests were graded, a teacher stood in front of the class and read out the names of the students who had passed. Of the twenty-five students in the room, only five heard their names—including Rudi, Gerta, and two of their friends, Eva and Inge. They received certificates entitling them to enroll in college.

Gerta had always dreamt of becoming a filmmaker but worried this might not be a practical way to make a living. She also liked the idea of being a doctor and decided to study medicine. Rudi's goal had never changed. He'd always been fascinated by chemistry and planned to study chemical engineering.

On the warm evening of September 18, 1945, Rudi, Gerta, Inge, and Eva met on a very crowded platform at the Bratislava railway station.

There was one more train due in that evening—the overnight to Prague, where the friends were headed for school. Everyone on the packed platform was waiting for that train. There'd never be room for all of them.

The Prague train approached, its engine pumping out clouds of black smoke. People pushed forward, determined to board.

But not quite as determined as Rudi and Gerta.

This journey was a new start for them. A new life after six years of war, six years of terror and loss. One way or another, they were getting on this train.

The friends quickly made a plan. Before the cars even stopped, Gerta and Eva would shove Rudi and Inge through an open door. Rudi and Inge would fight their way to a compartment and slide open the window, and Gerta and Eva would lift their luggage through the window and climb in.

The train slowed as it rolled into the station. Hot smoke swept over the platform. The crush of bodies tightened.

"Well," Gerta said. "Here we go."

Gerta and Rudi in Bratislava, Slovakia, 1944. *[Photo courtesy of the Association of Jewish Refugees/ Gerta Vrbova personal archive]*

THE STORY IS THE THING

ON JANUARY 21, 1985, RUDOLF Vrba walked to the witness stand in a crowded courtroom in Toronto, Canada. Sixty years old now, his black hair streaked with gray, Rudi addressed the court in fluent, accented English—his seventh language.

This was two weeks into the high-profile trial of a man named Ernst Zündel. A man who claimed the Holocaust—the systematic murder of Europe's Jews by the Nazis and their collaborators—never happened.

Born in Germany, Zündel had settled in Canada as young man and joined right-wing extremist groups. He set up a publishing house in his Toronto home and began distributing white supremacist and pro-Nazi books and pamphlets, including a work of his own entitled *The Hitler We Loved and Why*. Zündel declared the Holocaust to be a "Jewish hoax" and a "witch hunt." There had been no gas chambers at Auschwitz, he stated—or anywhere in Hitler's Europe.

How could anyone make such statements?

In the years since World War II, thousands of survivors have told the stories of what they witnessed and endured at the hands of the Nazis. We have the accounts of Allied soldiers who liberated the concentration camps, along with film footage and photographs, and rooms full of captured Nazi documents. We have engineering sketches and architectural plans used to build Hitler's killing centers.

We have the testimony of the perpetrators themselves. Beginning in November 1945 with the Nuremberg trials, SS guards and high-level Nazi officials testified in detail about their participation in mass shootings and murder in gas chambers. In 1946, the British arrested Rudolf Höss, the kommandant of Auschwitz. Höss made an exhaustively detailed confession, describing every step of the process of mass murder.

Construction crews at the site of Auschwitz—which is now a museum and memorial—have uncovered seven different diaries and notes buried during the war by Sonderkommando prisoners. These prisoners did not expect to survive and wanted the world to know what they'd seen. Their eyewitness accounts of the gas chambers match exactly with those of prisoners who survived, including Filip Müller.

Historians have determined that the Nazis killed a total of 6 million Jews during World War II, including 1.5 million children. The Holocaust is established fact. How can anyone disagree with a fact?

This is what Holocaust deniers do. This is what Ernst Zündel was doing.

Was it Zündel's legal right to tell such obvious lies? That was the question before the court. According to Canadian criminal code, it was illegal to spread what was called "false news." The law stated: "Everyone who willfully publishes a statement, tale or news that he knows is false and that causes or is likely to cause injury or mischief to a public interest is guilty of an indictable offense and is liable to imprisonment for two years."

A Holocaust survivor named Sabina Citron had filed a complaint, charging that Zündel had violated the false news law. Some in the Jewish community of Toronto and beyond did not agree with taking Zündel to court. A public trial, they argued, would only give the man a bigger stage for his ugly theatrics.

Citron countered that this downside was outweighed by the greater danger of silence. "Everyone knows what unchecked hate propaganda can lead to," she said. She especially wanted people who'd been in the camps to have the opportunity to confront Zündel's lies in public.

One of those who volunteered to testify was Rudolf Vrba.

Dr. Vrba, as the lawyers addressed him, explained to the jury that he was a professor of pharmacology at the University of British Columbia. His area of expertise was the chemistry of the human brain. He had lived and worked in Czechoslovakia, Israel, the United States, and Britain, before settling in Canada in 1967.

But Rudi was not in court to discuss his scientific career. He was there to bear witness to his experiences as a teenager during World War II.

Rudi described Auschwitz in detail. He described the selections on the railroad ramp, the trucks of people he watched being driven to the crematoria, the death of many friends, his own close calls and escape. He explained that when he visited his friend Fred Wetzler in the Birkenau mortuary, they could see, through the window of the shed, groups of people going into two of the crematorium buildings. They had a clear view of guards in gas masks dumping the contents of metal canisters through hatches in the roof.

Ernst Zündel's lawyer, Douglas Christie, launched into an aggressive cross-examination, suggesting that Rudi was misremembering details—or purposely misinterpreting them. The big brick crematorium buildings, for instance. "I put it to you," Christie said, "that the reason for those crematoria was to deal with the bodies of people who had died from typhus."

"This is ridiculous," Rudi replied.

"What?"

"This is a ridiculous statement."

And that was one of their more polite exchanges.

Christie proposed that just because more than a million people were seen going *into* the crematoria, that doesn't mean they died there.

"So it is possible that they are still there," Rudi fired back, "or that there is a tunnel, and they are now in China. Otherwise they were gassed."

"Well, tell me, sir," Christie demanded, "how did you know it was a gas chamber?"

"I knew that it is a gas chamber because I saw people going into the crematoria. I saw that they are not coming out. I heard that they are being gassed there, and I have seen Zyklon gas being thrown into the gas chamber. And therefore I concluded that it is not a kitchen or a bakery, but a gas chamber."

Christie tried another typical trick of Holocaust deniers—he challenged Rudi to produce a single Nazi autopsy of someone who'd been killed by poison gas. "Have you got that?"

Rudi explained that the SS did not register prisoners slated for extermination, let alone perform autopsies on them. "Your request, therefore, is nonsensical."

"Am I to take it, then, that *you* are the proof?" Christie shot back. "Is that it?"

"No, I am not the proof," Rudi said. "I am only one of those who recorded it for the first time when it was a big secret in 1944."

Back and forth they went, with Rudi likening Holocaust denial to other ignorant conspiracy theories—that the earth is flat, that the American moon landing was faked on a film set. "Judge Locke had his hands full," reported the Toronto *Globe and Mail*, "separating the verbal combatants."

At the end of the seven-week trial, Douglas Christie told the jury that the case was about freedom of speech—his client was merely expressing an alternative point of view. The jury didn't buy it and found him guilty of spreading damaging false news. Zündel's conviction was later overturned. Canada's Supreme Court struck down the "false news" law as unconstitutional, saying it "infringes the guarantee of freedom of expression." Zündel was later deported to Germany, where he died in 2017.

So—was it worth it?

Did Rudi Vrba accomplish anything by trading blows with a lawyer who took obvious glee in ridiculing Holocaust survivors? After all, Ernst Zündel may have been convicted, but he got what he wanted: a public forum for his lies.

Rudi was sure he'd done the right thing. The only way to fight big lies, he argued, was with aggressive doses of the truth.

The truth about World War II is staggering. The suffering was so vast, the numbers so large, that historians can only offer estimations. About fifteen million soldiers died in the European and Pacific theaters of the war. A much higher number of civilians were killed, forty million or more. Atrocities other than the Holocaust caused millions of these deaths. Japan's military and wartime government enslaved and starved millions of people in China and other parts of occupied Asia and the Pacific. Soviet secret police massacred Polish military officers and political opponents, and deported tens of thousands of men, women, and children from Latvia, Lithuania, and Estonia to prison camps in remote corners of the Soviet Union.

It's overwhelming. Far too much to fit in any one book. Any shelf of books.

To Rudolf Vrba, this was all the more reason to tell his story. One story about one teenager, he hoped, might help us to understand. To do better.

Rudi told his story in hundreds of lectures and interviews, in documentary films, and in his own autobiographical writings. He felt it was particularly vital to speak with young people. At a school talk in 1995, a student asked if Rudi thought the Holocaust could happen again.

"If it was possible yesterday, it's possible again," Rudi said, "unless we are vigilant."

Unfortunately, it was all too easy for Rudi to illustrate his point with examples of genocide from the second half of the twentieth century, including Cambodia in the mid-1970s and Rwanda in

1994. "If a proof was needed that the mentality and danger of the Holocaust are still with us, it's right there," he said.

That's the enemy, Rudi taught, the "mentality" of the Holocaust. This includes the conspiracy theories spread by people like Ernst Zündel—the invention of fake history to fit a hateful vision of the world. It includes the sick "reasoning" Auschwitz Kommandant Rudolf Höss used to explain his crimes—the twisted logic that allows one group of people to look on another group as fundamentally different, inferior, less worthy of rights.

"That's why it's so important," Rudi said, "that nobody gets away with racial hatred and lies."

In their own ways, Rudi's friends joined this lifelong struggle.

After fighting alongside Rudi in the Slovak anti-Nazi forces until the end of the war, Alfred Wetzler married a fellow Auschwitz survivor and worked as a journalist and editor in Czechoslovakia. He told the story of his wartime experience in the appropriately titled *Escape from Hell*. Wetzler died in 1988, at the age of sixty-nine.

Filip Müller was never comfortable with public speaking, never one to seek attention, but he stepped forward when his story needed to be heard. Müller testified at a trial of Auschwitz staff members in Germany in 1964, and gave a long, wrenching interview for the 1985 film *Shoah*, Claude Lanzmann's classic documentary about the Holocaust. One of the last survivors of the Sonderkommando, he spent fifteen years writing his own book, *Eyewitness Auschwitz*. Müller died in 2013, at the age of ninety-one.

Gerta Sidonová earned a medical degree in Prague, while Rudi got his doctorate in chemistry. They married in 1947 and had two daughters. Gerta and Rudi divorced in 1956, though they reestablished a friendship later in life, and Gerta kept the last name Vrbová.

In September 1958, during the heart of the Cold War, Gerta pulled yet off another daring escape, this time from the authoritarian rulers of communist Czechoslovakia. She wanted to move to Great Britain, but the Czech government did not allow its citizens to travel freely. It would not grant passports to Gerta's daughters.

"My wartime experience of crossing borders illegally and defying authority helped me not to give up hope," Gerta later said. "I believed that nothing is quite as impossible as it seems."

She told her daughters, ages four and six, to get ready for a hike. She packed a backpack and bundled the girls in warm clothes. They took a bus to a town at the base of the country's tallest mountain, rode chairlifts partway up the slope, and hiked through heavy rain over the summit and down muddy paths into Poland. They caught a train to Warsaw, where Gerta forged her daughters' names in her passport, then boarded a plane to Copenhagen, Denmark, and from there flew on to London.

Gerta remarried in Britain and had two more children. She enjoyed a successful career as a researcher and professor of neuroscience. For decades, she poured her energy into scientific work and her family, and rarely spoke of her wartime experiences. As she got older, though, she could foresee a time when there would be no Holocaust survivors alive to tell their stories. This inspired her to share her own survival story in a book, *Trust and Deceit*, and in talks at schools and museums. Gerta Vrbová died in London in 2020, at the age of ninety-three.

Rudi also remarried, and continued his research and teaching in Vancouver, Canada. Even in retirement, he continued giving talks and interviews. In 2005, a journalist named Paul McKay visited Rudi at home, and McKay's description of Rudi at eighty was remarkably similar to how Gerta described him at fifteen. "He has a hearty, wide smile," McKay wrote, "and a singsong way of speaking."

Rudi had just two "physical mementos" of Auschwitz, McKay noted. "The number 44070 tattooed on his arm, and the belt of a beloved, brave fellow prisoner."

This was Charles Unglick's belt, the now faded leather belt that Rudi had taken from Charlo's body after his failed escape attempt. Rudi wore it often in honor of his friend, and of many other lost friends. Rudolf Vrba died in Vancouver in 2006. He was eighty-one.

And now to end the book. But how?

This last little section was the hardest for me to write. I was convinced that I needed to think of some way to sum up this heartbreaking, infuriating, inspiring story. To give you some compact takeaway, some profound message to apply to daily life. I struggled with this for months.

The answer finally came from a conversation with a friend of Rudi's, Dr. Robert Krell, a colleague at the University of British Columbia. Dr. Krell survived the Holocaust as a young child in Holland and, on top of his academic work, has dedicated significant time and energy to Holocaust education.

"You saw Rudi speak, give presentations about his experiences— what would he say at the end?" I asked. "What did he want people to take away from his talks?"

Rudi didn't do that, Dr. Krell said. He didn't do your work for you.

The story is the thing; that's what Rudi would say. Everything is in the story.

You read the story. You know what to do.

Left: Watchtower at Birkenau.
Below, left and right: The Polish terrain Rudi and Fred covered, though of course they traveled by night. *[Photos by Steve Sheinkin]*

Above, left: On the hillside where the German patrol fired at Rudi and Fred.
Above, right: A short break in the Sola River. *[Photos by Jiří Němec]*

AUTHOR'S NOTE

EARLY ON THE MORNING OF August 1, 2022, I joined a group of about forty hikers at the gates of Birkenau. We wound our way around the camp complex, turned south, and started our journey across southern Poland. This was the Vrba-Wetzler Memorial, an annual trek (since 2014, minus a couple of Covid cancellations), a 140-kilometer march in the footsteps of the young heroes. For six days we hiked across meadows, through forests, over mountains, ending in Žilina, Slovakia, where we gathered in the basement room in which Rudi and Fred gave their testimony—the Auschwitz Protocol, more commonly known as the Vrba-Wetzler Report.

Of course, this was nothing like Rudi and Fred's escape. We walked openly along paths, stopped in stores, and slept in beds. Still, it was the most remarkable research trip of my life. Seeing the land and the distances. Literally feeling the slopes. Stopping to read aloud from Rudi and Fred's books at key spots along their route. Knowing my own ancestors, Jewish on both sides, had for generations lived not so far away. To the organizers and participants of the Vrba-Wetzler Memorial, thank you for welcoming me to the group, for patiently translating key information, and for sharing the journey.

For anyone researching Vrba's story, another essential stop is the Franklin D. Roosevelt Presidential Library and Museum in Hyde Park, New York, which houses the Rudolf Vrba Papers, a massive collection of letters, interview transcripts, newspaper clippings, and more. Thanks to Christian Belena for answering my questions and facilitating my visit.

I'm very grateful to Dr. Caroline Hilton, daughter of Gerta Vrbová from her second marriage, for sharing stories and photos of her mother. Thank you to Dr. Bea Lewkowicz, director of the Refugee Voices Testimony Archive at London's Association of Jewish Refugees. Dr. Lewkowicz knew both Gerta and Rudi, and provided me with a copy of the priceless photo on page 210. And thanks to Dr. Robert Krell for talking with me about what it was like to watch Rudi give lectures and interact with audiences. A huge thanks to Amanda Friedeman, assistant director of education at the Illinois Holocaust Museum, for reading a draft of this book and offering lots of useful corrections and suggestions.

And now the team—there's always a team. Thanks to everyone at Writers House, and particularly to Steven Malk, for his advice on telling this story. Thank you to my editor and collaborator Connie Hsu, who did so much to shape this book, helping to find the balance of storylines and context. Thanks to the entire Macmillan team: Nicolás Ore-Giron, Jen Healey, Sherri Schmidt, Aurora Parlagreco, Celeste Cass, Mary Van Akin, Kristin Luby, Elysse Villalobos, Grace Tyler, Morgan Kane, Tatiana Merced-Zarou, Jen Edwards, Allison Verost, and Jen Besser.

And, as always, I'm so grateful to Rachel, Anna, and David for listening to countless bits and pieces of this story, for saying "Yeah, that has to be in there" or "That's good, but it could be a blog post or something." This was a tough story to write, a difficult world to visit day after day. I couldn't have done it without you guys.

SOURCE NOTES

First, a note on names: Rudolf "Rudi" Vrba was born with the name Walter Rosenberg. He began using Rudi Vrba after his escape from Auschwitz and stuck with this new name for the rest of his life. In describing his own childhood and wartime experiences, he used the name Rudi. Gerta, in her recollections of those years, used the name Walter—that was how she knew him at the time. For the sake of clarity, and because it's what Rudi did in his own writings, I've used the name Rudi Vrba throughout this book.

The most valuable sources for this book were the firsthand accounts of the story's main figures: Rudolf Vrba, Gerta Vrbová, Filip Müller, and Alfred Wetzler. Vrba's sources include a remarkable book, *I Cannot Forgive*, first published in Britain in 1963, along with essays, interviews, and letters he exchanged with historians. Vrba's correspondence and other unpublished writings can be found in the Rudolf Vrba Papers at the Franklin D. Roosevelt Presidential Library and Museum in Hyde Park, New York.

Each source note below includes a key phrase, description, or quote, along with the page number on which the phrase, details, or quote appears. Subsequent quotes from the same conversation are from the same source, unless otherwise noted.

Prologue

ix   "Take care of yourself" and the start of Vrba's journey: Vrba, *I Cannot Forgive*, 23–24.

1

5   Rudi's childhood background: Vrba, *I Cannot Forgive*, 21; Vrba oral history, pt. 1.

6   Hitler's rise and antisemitism: Shirer, *Rise and Fall*, 250–71; Gilbert, *Holocaust*, 21–36.

6   Early Nazi concentration camps: Wachsmann, *KL*, 31–35, 96–104; Shirer, *Rise and Fall*, 272.

8   "My father said I shouldn't have come" and other memories of this scene: Vrbová, *Trust and Deceit*, 12–13.

2

10   Anti-Jewish laws in Slovakia: Kirschbaum, *History of Slovakia*, 196–97; Vrbová, *Trust and Deceit*, 18; Hilton-Vrbová oral history, pt. 1; Vrba, *I Cannot Forgive*, 21–22; Vrba oral history, pt. 1.

11 "Jews out" and Gerta's response: Hilton-Vrbová oral history, pt. 1; Vrbová, *Trust and Deceit*, 15.

11 "Don't worry. I've still got that chemistry book": Vrba, *I Cannot Forgive*, 62.

12 Meeting in meadow: Hilton-Vrbová oral history, pt. 1. "He had a round, friendly face": Vrbová, *Trust and Deceit*, 17.

13 "It will not be long now": Vrbová, *Trust and Deceit*, 19.

14 "For him I could do anything": Padfield, *Himmler*, 99.

3

15 "The Führer has given orders" and other details of Hitler's plans: Harding, *Hanns and Rudolf*, 112–13; Höss, *Death Dealer*, 27–28; Padfield, *Himmler*, 334; Rees, *Auschwitz*, 74.

16 Slovakia agrees to deport Jews: Kirschbaum, *History of Slovakia*, 198; Holocaust Encyclopedia, s.v. "Holocaust in Slovakia," encyclopedia.ushmm.org/content/en/article/the-holocaust-in-slovakia.

16 "Where do you think we will be sent?": Vrbová, *Trust and Deceit*, 21.

17 Rudi at Stefan's relatives' house: Vrba, *I Cannot Forgive*, 25–26.

4

19 "I suppose you know": Vrba, *I Cannot Forgive*, 26.

19 Conditions in Hungary: Cornelius, *Hungary in World War II*, 106–8; Eby, *Hungary at War*, 100; Braham, "Holocaust in Hungary," 33–34.

20 Rudi's capture and interrogation: Vrba, *I Cannot Forgive*, 28–29.

5

23 "Jesus, he's still alive": Vrba, *I Cannot Forgive*, 32–33.

24 "Mr. Jew": Vrba, *I Cannot Forgive*, 33.

24 Antisemitism in Europe: Sloyan, "Christian Persecution of Jews"; Gilbert, *Holocaust*, 19–20.

25 *Protocols of the Elders of Zion:* Holocaust Encyclopedia, s.v. "Protocols of the Elders of Zion," encyclopedia.ushmm.org/content/en/article/protocols-of-the-elders-of-zion; Zipperstein, "Conspiracy Theory."

25 "People will believe a big lie": Langer, *Psychological Analysis of Hitler*, 38.

26 Nováky and Rudi's first impressions: Vrba, *I Cannot Forgive*, 34–36; "Novaky," Holocaust Lexicon, Holocaust Resource Center, Yad Vashem, yadvashem.org/holocaust/resource-center/lexicon/n.html.

6

27 U.S. policy toward refugees: Brody, "American Jewry," 228–35; Library of Congress, "From Haven to Home."

28 "What will we do there?": Vrbová, *Trust and Deceit,* 23; Hilton-Vrbová oral history, pt. 1.

28 Rudi's escape from Nováky: Vrba, *I Cannot Forgive*, 34–37.

30 Rudi at Zuzka's house: Vrba, *I Cannot Forgive*, 39–40.

7

32 "If you had an old pair of shoes": Vrba, *I Cannot Forgive*, 41.

33 "Good afternoon. May I see your documents" and Rudi's capture: Vrba, *I Cannot Forgive*, 41.

34 "Please tell your father": Vrbová, *Trust and Deceit,* 27.

34 "We have to leave the house tonight": Vrbová, *Trust and Deceit,* 28.

35 "I felt in every fiber of my body": Vrbová, *Trust and Deceit,* 29.

8

36 "Try to escape again": Vrba, *I Cannot Forgive*, 45.

36 Details of the train ride: Vrba, *I Cannot Forgive*, 47–58; Vrba and Wetzler, *Extermination Camps of Auschwitz and*

Birkenau, 21 (hereafter Vrba-Wetzler Report); Vrba oral history, pt. 1. Additional prisoner train details: Wachsmann, *KL,* 307–8.

38 Einsatzgruppen killings: Gilbert, *Holocaust,* 217; Rhodes, *Masters of Death,* 38–42.

39 "To remove the anticipated multitudes": Padfield, *Himmler,* 334.

39 First gas chambers at Auschwitz: Höss, *Death Dealer,* 30–31; Gutman and Berenbaum, *Anatomy of Auschwitz,* 284–85; Rees, *Auschwitz,* 54–55; Wachsmann, *KL,* 267–70. Crematorium I still stands at the Auschwitz-Birkenau Memorial and Museum.

40 "I must admit openly": Höss, *Death Dealer,* 156.

9

43 Rudi's first impressions of Majdanek: Vrba, *I Cannot Forgive,* 60–62; Vrba-Wetzler Report, 22.

44 Majdanek details: Holocaust Encyclopedia, s.v. "Lublin/Majdanek Concentration Camp: Conditions," encyclopedia.ushmm.org/content/en/article/lublin-majdanek-concentration-camp-conditions; Wachsmann, *KL,* 319–20.

44 Camp routine, including colored triangles: Vrba-Wetzler Report, 2, 22–24; Vrba, *I Cannot Forgive,* 64–65; Wachsmann, *KL,* 125.

45 Rudi's determination to escape: Vrba oral history, pt. 2; Vrba, *Shoah* interview, pt. 1.

10

46 Gerta's life in Budapest, including buying matches: Vrbová, *Trust and Deceit,* 41–43; Hilton-Vrbová oral history, pt. 1.

48 Rudi works for Milan: Vrba, *I Cannot Forgive,* 68–69.

49 "You will be given food for the journey": Vrba, *I Cannot Forgive,* 72.

49 Rudi and Josef Erdelyi plan escape: Vrba, *I Cannot Forgive,* 73.

50 Auschwitz camp details: Dwork and Van Pelt. *Auschwitz,* 168–78; Holocaust Encyclopedia, s.v. "Auschwitz," encyclopedia.ushmm.org/content/en/article/auschwitz; "KL Auschwitz-Birkenau," History, Auschwitz-Birkenau Memorial and Museum, auschwitz.org/en/history/kl-auschwitz-birkenau/; Vrba-Wetzler Report, 2–3.

50 Rudi's first impressions of Auschwitz: Vrba, *I Cannot Forgive,* 75–76; Vrba-Wetzler Report, 24; Vrba oral history, pt. 2.

11

53 "I am entirely normal": G. M. Gilbert, *Nuremberg Diary* (New York: Farrar, Straus, 1947), 258, quoted in Harding, *Hanns and Rudolf,* 255.

53 The kommandant's house at Auschwitz: Friedrich, "The Kingdom of Auschwitz," 44; Harding, *Hanns and Rudolf,* 100–105.

54 "I had a razor in my hand": Rees, *Auschwitz,* 84.

54 Rudi's talk with Ipi Müller: Vrba, *I Cannot Forgive,* 79.

55 "Work makes life sweet!": Sarah Joskowitz, interview by Lillian Gewirtzman, New York, October 7, 1998, USC Shoah Foundation Visual History Archive, quoted in Harding, *Hanns and Rudolf,* 107.

55 Showers and tattoos: Vrba, *I Cannot Forgive,* 84–85; Dwork and Van Pelt, *Auschwitz,* 225.

56 "Let's have a look at you bastards!": Vrba, *I Cannot Forgive,* 87.

57 "You're lucky boys": Vrba, *I Cannot Forgive,* 89.

12

58 "This is the SS food store": Vrba, *I Cannot Forgive,* 92.

60 "Often my thoughts were far away": Vrbová, *Trust and Deceit,* 45.

60 Anti-Jewish laws in Hungary: Cornelius; *Hungary,* 106–7.

61 "They never asked about me": Vrbová, *Trust and Deceit*, 44; Hilton-Vrbová oral history, pt. 1.

62 Hanging of prisoners at Auschwitz: Vrba, *I Cannot Forgive*, 199–200.

13

65 Hitler's plans: Shirer, *Rise and Fall*, 913–16.

66 "Garden of Eden": Rees, *Auschwitz*, 46.

66 Nazi killing centers: Gilbert, *Holocaust*, 286; Wachsmann, KL, 322–25; Holocaust Encyclopedia, s.v. "Killing Centers: In Depth," encyclopedia.ushmm.org /content/en/article/killing-centers-in -depth.

67 the story "seemed too terrible": *New York Times*, "Allies Urged."

67 Roosevelt's Executive Order 9066: "Japanese American Internment," curriculum guide, FDR Library, fdrlibrary.org /curriculum-guide-internment; "Japanese American Incarceration," National World War II Museum, nationalww2museum .org/war/articles/japanese-american -incarceration.

68 "hold the perpetrators of these crimes": Pasley, "Jews Declare," *Daily News*.

68 "In a week's time": Vrba, *I Cannot Forgive*, 10.

69 Rudi's impressions of Himmler: Vrba, *I Cannot Forgive*, 14.

69 Himmler's 1942 visit to Auschwitz: Höss, *Death Dealer*, 32–33, 287; Wachsmann, KL, 289–90.

14

71 Prisoner population at Auschwitz: Gutman and Berenbaum, *Anatomy of Auschwitz*, 16–17; Wachsmann, KL, 340.

71 "How careless of me!": Vrba, *I Cannot Forgive*, 95.

72 "Lie down! Get up!" and tea incident: Müller, *Eyewitness Auschwitz*, 3; Müller, *Shoah* interview, 4–6.

74 "Get in, you swine!": Müller, *Shoah* interview, 6.

75 Müller's first day in Auschwitz crematorium: Müller, *Eyewitness Auschwitz*, 10–18; Müller, *Shoah* interview, 6–10.

15

77 Sonderkommando details: Holocaust Encyclopedia, s.v. "Sonderkommandos," encyclopedia.ushmm.org/content/en /article/sonderkommandos; "Sonderkommando," Holocaust Lexicon, Holocaust Resource Center, Yad Vashem, yadvashem.org/holocaust/resource-center /lexicon/s.html.

77 "You have come here to work": Müller, *Eyewitness Auschwitz*, 37; Müller, *Shoah* interview, 20–22.

78 "And what ought we prisoners": Müller, *Eyewitness Auschwitz*, 79.

79 "We were relieved of thinking": Langbein, *People in Auschwitz*, 283. For more of Stark's testimony and "reasoning," see Klee, *"Good Old Days,"* 252–55.

79 "Of course it was an unusual and monstrous order": Harding, *Hanns and Rudolf*, 114.

16

80 Franz throws marmalade to women: Vrba, *I Cannot Forgive*, 100.

81 "You're being transferred": Vrba, *I Cannot Forgive*, 106.

81 "Has everybody got bread?": Vrba, *I Cannot Forgive*, 107.

82 Rudi sent to Buna, conditions there: Vrba, *I Cannot Forgive*, 107–12; Vrba-Wetzler Report, 24–25; Vrba oral history, pt. 3.

17

86 Hitler's demands on Hungary: Cornelius, *Hungary*, 242–45.

87 "I, meanwhile, sat in the sun": Vrbová, *Trust and Deceit*, 46.

88 Ipi is dying: Vrba, *I Cannot Forgive*, 115.

88 Filip arranges meeting with Ipi: Müller, *Eyewitness Auschwitz*, 47; Müller, *Shoah* interview, 138–40.

88 Prisoners "organizing" goods: Vrba-Wetzler Report, 10; Vrba oral history, pt. 4.

89 "My father has told me": Vrba, *I Cannot Forgive*, 117.

89 Filip sees his father's body: Müller, *Eyewitness Auschwitz*, 48.

18

91 Typhus selection at Auschwitz: Vrba, *I Cannot Forgive*, 120–23.

91 Typhus in camp: "Sicknesses and Epidemics," History, Camp Hospitals, Auschwitz-Birkenau Memorial and Museum, auschwitz.org/en/history/camp-hospitals/sicknesses-and-epidemics/.

92 "You want to know what's happening?": Vrba, *I Cannot Forgive*, 124.

92 Rudi and Josef accepted into Canada Command: Vrba, *I Cannot Forgive*, 125–26.

19

94 Canada Command details: Rees, *Auschwitz*, 172–74; "The Auschwitz Album: 'Kanada,'" Yad Vashem, yadvashem.org/yv/en/exhibitions/album_auschwitz/kanada.asp; Vrba-Wetzler Report 25; Vrba, *Shoah* interview, 25–28.

94 Rudi's first impressions of Canada: Vrba, *I Cannot Forgive*, 127–30.

95 Wiegleb overseeing Canada: Vrba, *I Cannot Forgive*, 131.

97 Prisoners share supplies from Canada: Vrba, *I Cannot Forgive*, 132.

98 Massive theft at Nazi camps: Gutman and Berenbaum, *Anatomy of Auschwitz*, 245–62; Vrba-Wetzler Report, 26; Vrba, "Preparations," 65–66; Linn, *Escaping Auschwitz*, 17.

99 Bruno forces Rudi to deliver gifts: Vrba, *I Cannot Forgive*, 134.

20

100 Wiegleb catches Rudi: Vrba, *I Cannot Forgive*, 136–38.

101 "You did all right yesterday": Vrba, *I Cannot Forgive*, 139.

103 Stalingrad details: Shirer, *Rise and Fall*, 919; Beevor, *Stalingrad*, 187–207.

104 Changing conditions in Hungary: Cornelius; *Hungary*, 165, 184–86.

104 "We had to buy ration books": Vrbová, *Trust and Deceit*, 48.

21

105 "I can't bring you back to work": Vrba, *I Cannot Forgive*, 147.

105 Auschwitz railroad ramp details and selections: Vrba-Wetzler Report, 26; Vrba, "Personal Memories," 18–25; Vrba, "Preparations," 63–65; Wachsmann, *KL*, 307–12; "The Unloading Ramps and Selections," History, Auschwitz and Shoah, Auschwitz-Birkenau Memorial and Museum, auschwitz.org/en/history/auschwitz-and-shoah/the-unloading-ramps-and-selections/.

107 "Ladies and gentlemen, we are so sorry": Vrba oral history, pt. 1.

108 "One of those criminals": Vrba, *Shoah* interview, 20.

22

110 World War II update: Beevor, *Stalingrad*, 214–19; "Explore WWII History," National World War II Museum, nationalww2museum.org/students-teachers/student-resources/explore-wwii-history; Holocaust Encyclopedia, s.v. "World War II Timeline," encyclopedia.ushmm.org/content/en/article/world-war-ii-key-dates.

111 "Where the German soldier sets foot": Shirer, *Rise and Fall*, 919.

111 Josef taken to hospital and his death: Vrba, *I Cannot Forgive*, 157–58.

112 Rudi's bout with typhus: Vrba, *I Cannot Forgive*, 158–59.

114 Rudi finds the atlas: Vrba, "Preparations," 74; Vrba to Martin Gilbert, August 12, 1980, 12, Rudolf Vrba Papers.

23

116 Roosevelt and Churchill meet: Gilbert, *Holocaust*, 520; Overy, *Bombers and Bombed*, 107–9; Paul M. Sparrow, "The Casablanca Conference—Unconditional Surrender," *Forward with Roosevelt*, blog, January 10, 2017, FDR Library, fdr.blogs.archives.gov/2017/01/10/the-casablanca-conference-unconditional-surrender/.

116 German surrender at Stalingrad: Beevor, *Stalingrad*, 386–91.

117 "I need your help and support": Heinrich Himmler to Albert Ganzenmüller, January 20, 1943, International Military Tribunal, doc. NO-2405, quoted in Gilbert, *Holocaust*, 527.

117 "It is really you!": Vrba, *I Cannot Forgive*, 163.

118 Birkenau details, including gas chambers: Vrba-Wetzler Report, 5, 12; Vrba, *I Cannot Forgive*, 170–71; Vrba, "Preparations," 74; Gutman and Berenbaum, *Anatomy of Auschwitz*, 166–69.

119 Filip sees inside new crematorium: Müller, *Eyewitness Auschwitz*, 59–61; Müller, *Shoah* interview, 34–36. For design diagram, see Dwork and Van Pelt, *Auschwitz*, 322.

24

122 "Somehow, days that seemed endless": Vrbová, *Trust and Deceit*, 49.

122 Gerta and András: Vrbová, *Trust and Deceit*, 49–50.

123 "You'd better come with us": Vrbová, *Trust and Deceit*, 52.

124 Rudi connects with Fred Wetzler in Birkenau: Vrba, "Preparations," 72; Vrba, *I Cannot Forgive*, 172–73.

124 Wetzler describes his various jobs in camp: Vrba-Wetzler Report, 6–8. Morgue described: Wetzler, *Escape from Hell*, 46.

125 Rudi's new job: Vrba, "Preparations," 66–67; Vrba-Wetzler Report, 20.

125 Memorizing details: Vrba, "Preparations," 71; Vrba, *Shoah* interview, 52.

126 "Hitler will lose the war!": Müller, *Eyewitness Auschwitz*, 113.

25

127 "As regards the Jewish problem": Miklós Horthy to Pál Teleki, October 14, 1940, in *The Confidential Papers of Admiral Horthy*, eds. Miklós Szinai and László Szűcs (Budapest: Corvina Press, 1965), 150, quoted in Rabinovich, "How 'Anti-Semite' Saved Jews."

128 "I really let you down, Gerti": Vrbová, *Trust and Deceit*, 54; Hilton-Vrbová oral history, pt. 2.

128 "Perhaps I knew": Vrbová, *Trust and Deceit*, 58.

128 Dmitri's advice: Vrba, *I Cannot Forgive*, 204–5.

130 Rebellions at Treblinka and Sobibor: Holocaust Encyclopedia, s.v. "Killing Center Revolts," encyclopedia.ushmm.org/content/en/article/killing-center-revolts; Suhl, *They Fought Back*, 7–49, 128–34; Rashke, *Escape from Sobibor*, 295–320; Blatt, *Sobibor*, 74–82.

131 "This is a page of glory": Heinrich Himmler, speech at meeting of SS major generals in Posen, October 4, 1943, Harvard Law School Nuremberg Trials Project, nuremberg.law.harvard.edu/documents/3790.

26

132 Gerta goes to work for Baby: Vrbová, *Trust and Deceit*, 62.

133 "good times are coming": Vrba oral history, pt. 4. Rudi learns purpose of new rail line: Vrba, "Preparations," 68.

134 Rudi determined to escape soon: Vrba oral history, pt. 4.

134 Fero Langer's attempted escape: Müller, *Eyewitness Auschwitz*, 55–56; Vrba, *I Cannot Forgive*, 206–8.

135 "Three cheers, we've come back again!": Müller, *Eyewitness Auschwitz*, 56.

27

137 "You and I are going to get out": Vrba, *I Cannot Forgive*, 209.

138 Charles Unglick's attempted escape: Vrba, *I Cannot Forgive*, 212–15.

141 German troops invade Hungary, begin isolating Jews: Braham, *Politics of Genocide*, 99–103; Cornelius, *Hungary*, 277–94; Braham, "Holocaust in Hungary," 36–37.

141 "We knew our days in Budapest were numbered": Vrbová, *Trust and Deceit*, 65.

142 Rudi's evolving motivations: Vrba oral history, pt. 4; Vrba, "Preparations," 71; Vrba, *Shoah* interview, 6.

28

145 Auschwitz-Birkenau layout: Vrba-Wetzler Report, 3–4. For detailed diagrams, see Holocaust Encyclopedia, s.v. "Auschwitz—Animated Map," encyclopedia.ushmm.org/content/en/gallery/auschwitz-maps; Gilbert, *Auschwitz and the Allies*, 193, 195; Wachsmann, *KL*, 341.

147 Lumber pile escape idea: Vrba, *I Cannot Forgive*, 221; Vrba oral history, pt. 4.

149 Eisenbach captured: Vrba, *I Cannot Forgive*, 223.

29

151 "Do they know about it?": Vrba, *I Cannot Forgive*, 224.

152 "You must forgive me": Vrbová, *Trust and Deceit*, 65.

152 "This war will end soon": Vrbová, *Trust and Deceit*, 67.

153 Filip describes gas chamber details: Müller, *Eyewitness Auschwitz*, 68–69; Vrba-Wetzler Report, 12–13; Müller, *Shoah* interview, 110–12.

30

154 "Bring me back a pair of socks": Vrba, *I Cannot Forgive*, 225.

155 "What have we here?": Vrba, *I Cannot Forgive*, 226.

156 Rudi and Fred go into the wood pile: Vrba, *I Cannot Forgive*, 228; Wetzler, *Escape from Hell*, 108.

157 First hours in the pile: Vrba, *I Cannot Forgive*, 229–30; Wetzler, *Escape from Hell*, 110–11.

31

159 Filip's reaction to siren: Müller, *Eyewitness Auschwitz*, 120–21.

159 "Look behind those planks!": Vrba, *I Cannot Forgive*, 231.

160 Conditions in wood pile: Vrba, *I Cannot Forgive*, 232, Wetzler, *Escape from Hell*, 113.

161 "They can't have got away": Vrba, *I Cannot Forgive*, 232.

162 "Vacate guard posts!": Suhl, *They Fought Back*, 206.

162 "It could be a trick": Vrba, *I Cannot Forgive*, 234.

32

164 Rudi and Fred make it out of camp: Vrba, *I Cannot Forgive*, 234–35; Wetzler, *Escape from Hell*, 146–47.

166 ATTENTION! FORBIDDEN ZONE!: Gutman and Berenbaum, *Anatomy of Auschwitz*, 503.

167 Conditions in southern Poland: Gilbert, *Auschwitz and the Allies*, 196; Vrba, "Preparations," 74.

167 First hours outside of camp: Vrba, *I Cannot Forgive*, 236–37.

33

168 Allies bombing Hungary: Braham, *Politics of Genocide*, 101; Cornelius, *Hungary in World War II*, 288.

168 Gerta and Jozefina on the move: Vrbová, *Trust and Deceit*, 70–71.

169 Filip in Auschwitz: Müller, *Eyewitness Auschwitz*, 121–23.

169 Arrest warrant: Linn, *Escaping Auschwitz*, 20.

170 Rudi and Fred in park: Vrba, *I Cannot Forgive*, 238.

171 Getting lost near Bielsko: Vrba, *I Cannot Forgive*, 239; Vrba, "Preparations," 76–77.

34

173 "Praised be the name": Vrba, "Preparations," 76. Additional details of time at Polish women's house: Vrba, *I Cannot Forgive*, 239.

175 Gerta and Jozefina in Slovakia: Vrbová, *Trust and Deceit*, 76–80.

176 Rudi and Fred shot at by German patrol: Vrba, *I Cannot Forgive*, 241–42; Vrba, "Preparations," 76; Wetzler, *Escape from Hell*, 159–60.

35

178 "We're heading for the Slovak border": Vrba, *I Cannot Forgive*, 243.

179 "My grandmother will be back": Vrba, *I Cannot Forgive*, 243; Wetzler, *Escape from Hell*, 166–67.

180 Old man knows of arrest warrant: Wetzler, *Escape from Hell*, 175.

181 "Do exactly what I say": Vrba, *I Cannot Forgive*, 245.

182 Rudi and Fred cross the border: Vrba, *I Cannot Forgive*, 245.

36

184 Help from Andrej Čánecký: Vrba, *I Cannot Forgive*, 246–47; Vrba, "Preparations," 77–78.

185 Gerta joins Jewish underground: Vrbová, *Trust and Deceit*, 81–83.

186 "To hell with it": Vrba, *I Cannot Forgive*, 248.

186 "I've not much time": Vrba oral history, pt. 4; Vrba, "Preparations," 78.

187 "Tonight, you sleep at my place": Vrba, *I Cannot Forgive*, 248.

37

189 Meeting Jewish leaders in Žilina: Vrba, *I Cannot Forgive*, 248–50; Vrba, *Shoah* interview, 56–58; Vrba, "Preparations," 79–81. For specifics of their testimony, see Vrba-Wetzler Report.

190 "O.K. We'll go": "Research Starters: D-Day," Student Resources, National World War II Museum, nationalww2museum.org /students-teachers/student-resources /research-starters/research-starters-d-day.

191 Nazis deport Hungarian Jews: Braham, *Politics of Genocide*, 137–38; Cornelius, *Hungary*, 298.

191 "Why did I escape?": Vrba, *I Cannot Forgive*, 251.

192 Vrba-Wetzler Report details: Vrba and Wetzler, *Extermination Camps of Auschwitz and Birkenau*; Robert Rozett, introduction to Wetzler, *Escape from Hell*, xi.

192 Roosevelt and others pressure Horthy: Braham, *Politics of Genocide*, 161.

192 Horthy halts deportation: Gutman and Berenbaum, *Anatomy of Auschwitz*, 551; Braham, *Politics of Genocide*, 163.

193 "No other single act": Martin Gilbert, foreword to Wetzler, *Escape from Hell*, vii.

38

195 "There were times when we wondered": Vrba, *I Cannot Forgive*, 254.

195 "Would you like to see him?": Vrbová, *Trust and Deceit*, 84.

196 Gerta sees Rudi again: Vrbová, *Trust and Deceit*, 86; Hilton-Vrbová oral history, pt. 2.

196 "What are you staring at?": Vrbová, *Trust and Deceit*, 88.

197 Majdanek details, including gas chambers: Wachsmann, *KL*, 321; Holocaust Encyclopedia, s.v. "Lublin/Majdanek Concentration Camp: Conditions."

197 "I have just seen the most terrible place": W. H. Lawrence, "Nazi Mass Killing," *New York Times*.

197 Hitler's deteriorating condition: Shirer, *Rise and Fall*, 1102.

198 Rudi joins partisan fighters: Vrba, *I Cannot Forgive*, 260–61; Vrba oral history, pt. 5; Vrba, "Preparations," 87.

39

199 "Open up! This is the Gestapo!": Vrbová, *Trust and Deceit*, 94. Hilton-Vrbová oral history, pt. 2.

200 "Would you like an apple?": Vrbová, *Trust and Deceit*, 98.

200 Gerta and Jozefina talk in prison: Vrbová, *Trust and Deceit*, 106, 114.

202 Gerta's escape: Vrbová, *Trust and Deceit*, 115–20; Hilton-Vrbová oral history, pt. 2.

40

204 Gerta returns to Hungary: Vrbová, *Trust and Deceit*, 130; Hilton-Vrbová oral history, pt. 3.

204 Nazis evacuate Auschwitz: Gilbert, *Auschwitz and the Allies*, 334–36; Holocaust Encyclopedia, s.v. "Auschwitz."

205 Filip's description of evacuation and march: Müller, *Eyewitness Auschwitz*, 162–67; Müller, *Shoah* interview, 133.

205 "We are free!": Müller, *Eyewitness Auschwitz*, 171.

205 Himmler captured: Padfield, *Himmler*, 608–10; Rhodes, *Masters of Death*, 272.

206 Gerta returns to Trnava: Vrbová, *Trust and Deceit*, 174; Vrbová, *Betrayed Generation*, 16–22; Hilton-Vrbová oral history, pt. 3.

208 "We hardly slept at all": Vrbová, *Betrayed Generation*, 27.

209 Gerta and Rudi leave for Prague: Vrbová, *Betrayed Generation*, 30–31.

Epilogue

211 Zündel trial background: Weimann and Winn, *Hate on Trial*, 13–19.

212 Höss arrest: Höss, *Death Dealer*, 178.

212 Sonderkommando notes found: Gilbert, *Holocaust*, 820; Wachsmann, *KL*, 352.

213 "Everyone knows what unchecked hate": Weimann and Winn, *Hate on Trial*, 30.

213 Vrba's trial testimony: Her Majesty the Queen v. Ernst Zundel, complete court transcript, District Court of Ontario, Toronto, January 7, 1985, 1244–1641.

215 "Judge Locke had his hands full" and Zündel's conviction: Kirk Makin's series of articles in the *Globe and Mail*, including "Zundel Guilty," March 1, 1985; Tingler, "Holocaust Denial," 220.

216 World War II deaths, atrocities: Holocaust Encyclopedia, s.v. "Documenting Numbers of Victims of the Holocaust and Nazi Persecution," encyclopedia.ushmm .org/content/en/article/documenting -numbers-of-victims-of-the-holocaust -and-nazi-persecution; "Research Starters: Worldwide Deaths in World War II," Student Resources, National World War II Museum, nationalww2museum .org/students-teachers/student-resources /research-starters/research-starters -worldwide-deaths-world-war; U.S. National Archives, "Records Katyn Forest Massacre."

216 "If it was possible yesterday": Schultz, "Auschwitz Escapee Tells Students," *Forecaster*.

217 "If a proof was needed": Adler, "Human Rights Warrior," *Vancouver Sun*.

217 "That's why it's so important": Adler, "Escape from Auschwitz," *Edmonton Journal*.

217 Wetzler's postwar life: Richman, "Two Friends."

217 Filip Müller details: Kilian, "In Memoriam: Filip Müller."

218 "My wartime experience": Vrbová, *Trust and Deceit*, 179.

218 Gerta's later years: Hilton, "Gerta Vrbová Obituary," *Guardian*.

219 "He has a hearty, wide smile": McKay, "Escape from Auschwitz," *Ottawa Citizen*. Rudi's belt is now on display at the Imperial War Museum in London.

219 Dr. Krell on Rudi's presentations: Robert Krell, interview by author.

BIBLIOGRAPHY

Firsthand Accounts

Hilton, Caroline. Interview by author, November 4, 2021.

Hilton-Vrbová, Gerta. Oral history interview by Lyn Smith, April 15, 2003. Audio, four parts. Sound Archive, Imperial War Museum, London.

Höss, Rudolf. *Death Dealer: The Memoirs of the SS Kommandant at Auschwitz*. Edited by Steven Paskuly. Translated by Andrew Pollinger. New York: Da Capo Press, 1996.

Krell, Robert. Interview by author, January 13, 2022.

Müller, Filip. *Eyewitness Auschwitz: Three Years in the Gas Chambers*. Edited and translated by Susanne Flatauer. Chicago: Ivan R. Dee, 1999. Published in association with the United States Holocaust Memorial Museum.

Müller, Filip. Interview by Claude Lanzmann, Germany, spring 1979, for film *Shoah* (1985). Transcript translated by Uta Allers. Claude Lanzmann *Shoah* Collection, United States Holocaust Memorial Museum.

Vrba, Rudolf. "Footnote to the Auschwitz Report." *Jewish Currents*, March 1966, 22–23.

Vrba, Rudolf. Interview by Claude Lanzmann, New York, November 1978, for film *Shoah* (1985). Transcript. Claude Lanzmann *Shoah* Collection, United States Holocaust Memorial Museum.

Vrba, Rudolf. Oral history interview by Thames Television, 1972, for "Genocide, 1941–1945," episode 20 of *The World at War* (1974). Audio, five parts. Jeff and Toby Herr Oral History Archive, United States Holocaust Memorial Museum.

Vrba, Rudolf. Letters to Martin Gilbert, 1942–2001. Box 2, Rudolf Vrba Papers, 1934–2008, Franklin D. Roosevelt Presidential Library and Museum.

Vrba, Rudolf. "Personal Memories of Actions of SS Doctors of Medicine in Auschwitz I and Auschwitz II (Birkenau)," 1989–1992, undated. Box 9, Rudolf Vrba Papers, 1934–2008, Franklin D. Roosevelt Presidential Library and Museum.

Vrba, Rudolf. "The Preparations for the Holocaust in Hungary: An Eyewitness Account." In Braham and Miller, *Nazis' Last Victims*, 55–101.

Vrba, Rudolf, and Alan Bestic. *I Cannot Forgive*. London: Sidgwick and Jacks, 1963.

Vrba, Rudolf, and Alfred Wetzler. *The Extermination Camps of Auschwitz (Oświęcim) and Birkenau in Upper Silesia*, June 1944. Translated by Roswell D. McClelland. Box 7, Records of the War Refugee Board, Franklin D. Roosevelt Presidential Library and Museum. Known as the Vrba-Wetzler Report.

Vrbová, Gerta. *Betrayed Generation: Shattered Hopes and Disillusion in Post-War Czechoslovakia.* Cambridge, UK: Zuza Books, 2010.

Vrbová, Gerta. Interview 220, April 2019. Summary. Refugee Voices, Testimony Archive of the Association of Jewish Refugees.

Vrbová, Gerta. *Trust and Deceit: A Tale of Survival in Slovakia and Hungary, 1939–1945.* Edgware, UK: Vallentine Mitchell, 2006.

Wetzler, Alfred. *Escape from Hell: The True Story of the Auschwitz Protocol.* Edited by Péter Várnai-Wetzler. Translated by Ewald Osers. New York: Berghahn Books, 2007.

Secondary Sources: Books, Magazines, Journals

Beevor, Antony. *Stalingrad: The Fateful Siege, 1924–1943.* New York: Penguin Books, 1998.

Blatt, Thomas (Toivi). *Sobibor: The Forgotten Revolt.* Issaquah, WA: H.E.P., 1998.

Borhi, László. "The Allies, Secret Peace Talks, and the German Invasion of Hungary, 1943–1944." *Hungarian Studies Review* 46–47, no. 1 (2020): 89–100.

Braham, Randolph L. "The Holocaust in Hungary: A Retrospective Analysis." In Braham and Miller, *Nazis' Last Victims,* 27–43.

Braham, Randolph L. *The Politics of Genocide: The Holocaust in Hungary.* Condensed edition. Detroit: Wayne State University Press, 2000.

Braham, Randolph L., and Scott Miller, eds. *The Nazis' Last Victims: The Holocaust in Hungary.* Detroit: Wayne State University Press, 1998. Published in association with the United States Holocaust Memorial Museum.

Brody, David. "American Jewry, the Refugees and Immigration Restriction (1932–1942)." *Publications of the American Jewish Historical Society* 45, no. 4 (June 1956): 219–47.

Cornelius, Deborah S. *Hungary in World War II: Caught in the Cauldron.* New York: Fordham University Press, 2011.

Dwork, Debórah, and Robert Jan van Pelt. *Auschwitz: 1270 to the Present.* New York: W. W. Norton, 1997.

Eby, Cecil D. *Hungary at War: Civilians and Soldiers in World War II.* University Park: Pennsylvania State University Press, 1998.

Friedrich, Otto. "The Kingdom of Auschwitz." *Atlantic,* September 1981, 30–60.

Gilbert, Martin. *Auschwitz and the Allies.* New York: Henry Holt, 1982.

Gilbert, Martin. *The Holocaust: A History of the Jews of Europe During the Second World War.* New York: Holt, Rinehart, and Winston, 1985.

Greif, Gideon. *We Wept Without Tears: Testimonies of the Jewish Sonderkommando from Auschwitz.* New Haven, CT: Yale University Press, 2005.

Gutman, Yisrael, and Michael Berenbaum. *Anatomy of the Auschwitz Death Camp.* Bloomington: Indiana University Press, 1994. Published in association with the United States Holocaust Memorial Museum.

Harding, Thomas. *Hanns and Rudolf: The True Story of the German Jew Who Tracked Down and Caught the Kommandant of Auschwitz.* New York: Simon & Schuster, 2013.

Henry, Patrick, ed. *Jewish Resistance Against the Nazis.* Washington, DC: Catholic University of America Press, 2014.

Kilian, Andreas. "In Memoriam: Filip Müller." Translated by Peter Lande. *Holocaust and Genocide Studies* 29, no. 2 (Fall 2015): 348–50.

King, David. *The Trial of Adolf Hitler: The Beer Hall Putsch and the Rise of Nazi Germany.* New York: W. W. Norton, 2017.

Kirschbaum, Stanislav J. *A History of Slovakia: The Struggle for Survival.* New York: Palgrave Macmillan, 1995.

Klee, Ernst, Willi Dressen, and Volker Riess, eds. *"The Good Old Days": The Holocaust as Seen by Its Participants and Bystanders.* New York: Free Press, 1988.

Langbein, Hermann. *People in Auschwitz.* Translated by Harry Zohn. Chapel Hill: University of North Carolina Press, 2004.

Langer, Walter C. *A Psychological Analysis of Adolf Hitler.* Washington, DC: Office of Strategic Services, [1943?].

Lanzmann, Claude. *Shoah: The Complete Text of the Acclaimed Holocaust Film.* New York: Da Capo Press, 1995.

Laqueur, Walter. *The Terrible Secret: Suppression of the Truth About Hitler's "Final Solution."* New York: Penguin Books, 1982.

Linn, Ruth. *Escaping Auschwitz: A Culture of Forgetting.* Ithaca, NY: Cornell University Press, 2004.

Lipstadt, Deborah. *Denying the Holocaust: The Growing Assault on Truth and Memory.* New York: Plume Books, 1994.

Mansky, Jackie. "Why It Matters That Hungary's Prime Minister Denounced His Country's Role in the Holocaust." *Smithsonian Magazine,* July 21, 2017.

Overy, Richard. *The Bombers and the Bombed: Allied Air War over Europe, 1940–1945.* New York: Viking, 2013.

Padfield, Peter. *Himmler: Reichsführer-SS.* London: Macmillan, 1990.

Rabinovich, Eliezer M. "How 'Anti-Semite' Miklos Horthy Saved the Jews of Budapest." With Rachel Gross. *Moment,* October 9, 2014.

Rashke, Richard. *Escape from Sobibor.* Harrison, NY: Delphinium Books, 2012.

Rees, Laurence. *Auschwitz: A New History.* New York: Public Affairs, 2005.

Rhodes, Richard. *Masters of Death: The SS-Einsatzgruppen and the Invention of the Holocaust.* New York: Alfred A. Knopf, 2002.

Richman, Jackson. "Two Friends Who Escaped from Auschwitz and Warned the World." *Tablet Magazine,* April 11, 2018.

Shirer, William L. *The Rise and Fall of the Third Reich: A History of Nazi Germany.* New York: Simon & Schuster, 1960.

Sloyan, Gerard S. "Christian Persecution of Jews over the Centuries." United States Holocaust Memorial Museum, ushmm.org/m/pdfs/20070119-persecution.pdf.

Suhl, Yuri, ed. and trans. *They Fought Back: The Story of the Jewish Resistance in Nazi Europe.* New York: Shocken, 1975.

Tingler, Jason. "Holocaust Denial and Holocaust Memory: The Case of Ernst Zündel." *Genocide Studies International* 10, no. 2 (Fall 2016): 210–29.

United States Holocaust Memorial Museum. *Days of Remembrance, April 3–10, 1994: Fifty Years Ago, Darkness Before Dawn; Planning Guide for Commemoration Programs.* Washington, DC: United States Holocaust Memorial Museum, 1994.

Wachsmann, Nikolaus. *KL: A History of the Nazi Concentration Camps.* New York: Farrar, Straus and Giroux, 2015.

Weimann, Gabriel, and Conrad Winn. *Hate on Trial: The Zundel Affair, the Media, and Public Opinion in Canada.* Oakville, ON: Mosaic Press, 1986.

Zipperstein, Steven J. "The Conspiracy Theory to Rule Them All." *Atlantic,* August 25, 2020.

Newspaper Articles

Adler, Peter. "Escape from Auschwitz." *Edmonton Journal* (Alberta), April 2, 1989.

Adler, Peter. "Human Rights Warrior." *Vancouver Sun* (British Columbia), April 5, 2001.

Associated Press. "Auschwitz Commandant's Barber Jozef Paczynski Dies Aged 95." *Guardian* (London), April, 2015.

Brigham, Daniel T. "Inquiry Confirms Nazi Death Camps." *New York Times*, July 3, 1944.

Brigham, Daniel T. "Two Death Camps Places of Horror." *New York Times*, July 6, 1944.

Brooklyn Eagle. "Rally of 20,000 Denounces Axis for Atrocities." July 22, 1942.

Grant, Susan. "Holocaust Honoree Vrba Says He's No Hero." *Detroit Jewish News*, November 17, 1989.

Hawthorn, Tom. "Witness to Auschwitz." *Province* (Vancouver, BC), April 24, 1994.

Hilton, Caroline. "Gerta Vrbova Obituary." *Guardian* (London), October 19, 2020.

Independent Jewish Press Service. "F. R. Promises Nazis 'Day of Reckoning.'" *American Jewish World* (Minneapolis), July 24, 1942.

Jewish Western Bulletin (Vancouver, BC). "Vrba Views Vigilance as Vital for Jewish Future." September 7, 1989.

Lawrence, W. H. "Nazi Mass Killing Laid Bare in Camp." *New York Times*, August 30, 1944.

Makin, Kirk. "Escaper Tells of Arrivals in Auschwitz." *Globe and Mail* (Toronto), January 22, 1985.

Makin, Kirk. "Fists, Eggs Thrown as Zundel Trial Starts." *Globe and Mail* (Toronto), January 8, 1985.

Makin, Kirk. "Holocaust Survivor Is Accused of Lying by Zundel Lawyer." *Globe and Mail* (Toronto), January 25, 1985.

Makin, Kirk. "Lawyer and Holocaust Survivor Tangle at Publisher's Trial." *Globe and Mail* (Toronto), January 24, 1985.

Makin, Kirk. "Zundel Guilty, but Unrepentant." *Globe and Mail* (Toronto), March 1, 1985.

Martin, Douglas. "Rudolf Vrba, 81, Auschwitz Witness, Dies." *New York Times*, April 7, 2006.

May, Jeanne. "Holocaust Center Honors Canadian." *Detroit Free Press*, November 13, 1989.

McKay, Paul. "Escape from Auschwitz." *Ottawa Citizen*, May 6, 2005.

New York Times. "Allies Are Urged to Execute Nazis." July 2, 1942.

New York Times. "Czechs Report Massacre." June 20, 1944.

New York Times. "11 Allies Condemn Nazi War on Jews." December 18, 1942.

Pasley, Fred. "Jews Declare 5,000,000 Face a Nazi Death," *Daily News* (New York), December 9, 1942.

Retter, Emily. "We Survived the Holocaust Apart." *Mirror* (London). May 3, 2014.

Schultz, Harriet B. "Auschwitz Escapee Tells Students Holocaust Could Happen Again." *Forecaster* (Falmouth, ME), April 6, 1995.

United Press. "1,000,000 Jews Slain by Nazis, Report Says." *New York Times*, June 30, 1942.

Online Sources and Archives

For background information on events, Nazi camps, oral histories, and more:

Auschwitz-Birkenau Memorial and Museum, Oświęcim, Poland, auschwitz.org/en.

Franklin D. Roosevelt Presidential Library and Museum, Hyde Park, NY, fdrlibrary.org.

Imperial War Museum, London, iwm.org.uk.

Jewish Virtual Library, jewishvirtuallibrary.org.

Library of Congress. "From Haven to Home: 350 Years of Jewish Life in America." Exhibition, September 9–December 30, 2004, loc.gov/exhibits/haventohome.

National World War II Museum, New Orleans, nationalww2museum.org.

U.S. Holocaust Memorial Museum, Washington, DC, ushmm.org.

U.S. National Archives and Records Administration. "Records Relating to the Katyn Forest Massacre at the National Archives." Last reviewed November 25, 2022, archives.gov/research/foreign-policy/katyn-massacre.

Yad Vashem: The World Holocaust Remembrance Center, Jerusalem, Israel, yadvashem.org.

INDEX